A CHILD'S WALK
IN THE WILDERNESS

Venado
(Asher)

To Isabel

Welcome to the
Barbarian Utopia!

[signature]

A CHILD'S WALK IN THE WILDERNESS

An 8-Year-Old Boy and His Father
Take on the Appalachian Trail

Paul Molyneaux
Illustrations by Asher Molyneaux

STACKPOLE
BOOKS

Published by
STACKPOLE BOOKS
5067 Ritter Road
Mechanicsburg, PA 17055
www.stackpolebooks.com

Printed in U.S.A.

10 9 8 7 6 5 4 3 2 1

First edition

Cover design by Wendy A. Reynolds

Library of Congress Cataloging-in-Publication Data

Molyneaux, Paul.
  A child's walk in the wilderness : an 8-year-old boy and his father take on the Appalachian trail / Paul Molyneaux.
     p. cm.
  ISBN 978-0-8117-1178-4
  1. Hiking—Appalachian Trail. 2. Fathers and sons—Appalachian Trail. 3. Family recreation—Appalachian Trail. I. Title.
  GV199.42.A68M65 2013
  796.510974—dc23
                                        2012034305

To my brother Jim
1956–2012

Contents

1

THE FLOOD

"Water at high level forms a high potential pressure, and the result of its release depends upon the sluiceway. If this be intact the flow becomes controlled and its power made constructive; if weak and leaky the power peters out or spreads disaster. As with water pressure so with soul pressure: its 'hydraulics' are the same. The Puritan would build a dam; but the Barbarian would build a sluiceway."

—Benton MacKaye, from the "Barbarian Utopia" speech given before the New England Trail Conference, January 21, 1927

Rain splatters against the side of the outhouse at Pogo Campsite, where my son and I have found shelter from the easterly winds and steady rain. Inside, with our gear jammed into the corners and our hastily struck tent dripping on the floor, I take boiling water from a small alcohol stove and pour it into a pouch of freeze-dried huevos rancheros.

"I think we're going to need a hot breakfast today," I tell my son, Venado—it's his trail name, Spanish for "deer." Seven years old, he stands on the toilet seat, poking at a spiderweb with a stick, and knocking debris down into our food.

"Whoa, Venado, what are you doing?" I ask, looking up at him.

"Just playing."

"You're not *just* playing," I say. "You're polluting. Now pay attention—this is our precious food."

As I pack our gear, Venado carefully ties his boots and then puts on the gaiters he wears over them. He slips his belt through the loops that hold up his bright red rain chaps, and dons a heavy rain jacket, hat, neck warmer, and gloves. It's a lot to deal with and I help him with all

1

the lacing and zippers and Velcro. We fit a garbage bag over his small pack, and I lift it so he can find the shoulder straps.

"I can do it," he protests.

"Yeah, yeah," I laugh. "Come on."

Out in the weather the wind-driven rain finds the gaps in our gear. Venado's jacket does not cover the tops of his rain chaps and the rain drips down onto his pants. I'm wearing a twenty-five-cent emergency poncho I bought the year before in Phnom Penh; it's more idea than function, and the heavy linen shirt and cotton T-shirt I wear underneath it go from damp to soaked in the first mile.

Along the way Venado complains about a sore spot on his foot. Working quickly, I unpack our first-aid kit and cut a strip of moleskin—thin felt with an adhesive back. I untie Venado's boot, pull down the sock, and press the moleskin down on a growing blister. "That it?"

"Yeah."

"Your feet staying dry?"

"Mmhmm."

I retie the lock knot above the instep on his boot a little looser this time and take a double wrap around the last hooks at the top and finish it off with a double knot. After four days of patching blisters we have the drill down, but it still takes time.

"Are you warm?" I ask, shivering a little.

"Yeah. Are you?"

"I will be as long as we keep moving."

We march on, punching through patches of knee-deep snow and picking our way along rock-strewn ridgelines. "Some people don't think walking in the rain is very fun," says Venado, stopping and looking at the mist blowing between the trees. "But look at all that fog down there; it's actually quite pretty. Walking in the rain is lots of fun."

"I think we're in a cloud," I tell him.

"A cloud?"

"Fog doesn't happen in the wind, and we're high up, in a cloud."

He takes that in and skips along down the trail, until we hit more snow.

We carry a segment of pages torn from the Appalachian Long Distance Hikers Association's *Thru-Hikers' Companion*—a compilation of critical information about the trail. Our pages cover the route from Harpers Ferry to Vermont.

"It says there's a hostel five miles from Pogo, but it doesn't open until March fifteenth."

"What's today?"

"The twelfth. Maybe we'll be lucky."

Venado spots a herd of deer leaping through a thicket of thorny vines that he and I call "Cambodian rain gear destroyer" because, hemming the trail, it has torn my cheap poncho to shreds.

"There you go, Venado, you saw your animal."

"But we haven't seen an owl," he says, in reference to my trail name, Tecolote—Mexican Spanish for "owl."

"No, not yet."

We descend onto the road. After the snow and rock of the trail, the strip of smooth black tar passing through the wet forest affords us some easy walking. We double-check the guidebook. "One-third of a mile west."

It's a long third of a mile, as we search for the Free State Hikers Hostel, having no idea what it looks like or even what side of the road it's on. Eventually Venado spots a small white sign on a tree in front of an unremarkable suburban house: "Free State." It's not actually free, but it's dry, and the owner, Ken "Bone-Pac" Berry, a former thru-hiker, lets us in. Venado goes barefoot through the carpeted rooms and plays air hockey with Berry's daughter while I do laundry, throwing every-thing—even the tent—into the dryer. We bask in the warmth and comfort, and I don't ask the price until the next morning.

Berry tallies our bill. "It's thirty-two dollars for you and for kids we charge by the age. How old are you, Venado?"

"Seven."

"So that's thirty-nine dollars, plus two Pepsis. Forty-one dollars."

It's over our budget, but worth it, and I hand him two damp, dirty twenties and four quarters. "Oh, I love this trail money," says Berry, smiling as he smoothes the crumpled bills. He tells us how, after his thru-hike, he wanted to stay connected to the trail, so he and his wife bought this house and turned it into a hostel.

Outside, the rain pours down, one of those long, drenching rains that rolls in warm from the sea and washes all the snow off the mountains. Though tempted to stay another night at the hostel, we decide to hike on, quoting the thru-hiker's motto: "No rain, no pain, no Maine."

But we procrastinate over details and decide to weigh our packs. Standing on the scale I heft them one at a time and do the math, subtracting my unburdened weight from that with the pack. Venado's comes in at 14 pounds, a couple of pounds over the ideal 20 percent of body weight for a 60-pound boy. Mine too comes in over the 20 percent target—28 pounds for a 135-pound man.

"As soon as we eat a couple of meals we'll be light enough," I tell Venado.

Resolute, we don our ponchos, shoulder our packs, and head for the woods.

"There's some streams you have to cross," Berry says, with an air of uncertainty. "They may be running high."

Venado and I nod and step out the door. A half mile up the trail we hit the first of those streams, gorged with meltwater and roaring down a steep hill. I look it over, shaking my head. "I don't know, Venado. I think we might have to go back to the Free State."

"No, no," says my little boy, pointing further upstream. "We can cross up there, on that log, see?"

"Oh yeah. Okay." I tap him lightly on the shoulder, prodding him forward. "Let's go; we'll give it a try."

We cross the wide log onto a small island and find only a thin tree fallen across the second branch of the stream. The bark has peeled off, and muddy water surges under, and sometimes over, the shiny wet wood.

"Let's have your pack," I say. Venado slips his pack off and watches as I lean back and wing it across to the other side. "There," I tell him, "now we have to go."

Finding a stick and using it for support, I cross the log first. On the far side I turn and see Venado with one foot on the log, preparing to follow. "Wait!" I holler, holding up my hand. Deeper in the woods I find a long, thin dead tree and drag it up to the bank. Working one end across to Venado, I point to a tree with a split trunk. "Wedge it into that tree there," I shout over the roaring brook, and we succeed in improvising a handrail. "Don't lean on it; just use it for balance," I holler to Venado, and he crosses, one hand lightly on the rail, carefully placing each step of his wet boots on the slick wood. I watch his feet, poised to jump if it comes to that—but it doesn't.

"Well I guess we crossed the Rubicon," I say, once he reaches terra firma.

"What's the Rubicon?" he asks as I help him with his pack.

"It means we're not going back."

We hike on, splashing through the meltwater that has literally turned the trail into a sluiceway.

"We should call this the Appalachian River." ˡ

"Yeah."

Every little trickle of a stream has spread out across the forest floor, compelling us to bushwhack around extensive puddles. Our path crosses an open field where the sodden ground sucks at our boots and the wind blows the rain into our faces.

"Walk close behind me, Venado. We're almost back to the woods."

Coming down a hill we can hear roaring and see a boiling stream. "Looks like big water."

"How will we cross?"

A red pickup truck scrambles up a washed-out road on the other side of the stream, and the drift of the road tends closer to the bank as it runs downhill. Trusting our intuition, we follow deer trails downstream until we find a bridge. We cross, but the road on the other side is a mess, cut with deep trenches and water over our boot tops. We make our way along the embankment back to the white blazes—the six-inch by two-inch white marks painted on trees, rocks, and other immovable objects that mark the trail from Georgia to Maine.

Venado, unfazed by the difficulties, peppers me with questions, as he has done since we left Harpers Ferry five days ago: "What's the longest time you've been out in the woods? How far did you hike? What's the highest mountain you climbed? How high is Mount Katahdin? What's the highest mountain in the world? Who won at Gettysburg? Who shot Stonewall Jackson?"

"He was shot by his own men, a bunch of nervous guys from North Carolina, so they say."

Back at the hostel, I had mentioned the constant barrage of questions to my wife. "I thought about shutting off the questions," I'd said to her on the phone. "But then I figured, why not let him go on? I figure he'll run out after a while."

"He may not," said Venado's remarkably prescient mother.

Two miles past the bridge we hear the roaring again, and, drawing closer, we can see a fat brown ribbon of muddy water undulating in the trees. Raven Run, swollen with a winter's worth of melted snow and two days of rain, has jumped its banks at the bottom of the shallow valley and inundated the woods. The trail disappears underwater still fifty yards from the main current. Only a mile from our day's destination, we find ourselves stymied.

"What will we do, Poppy?"

"I don't know. This doesn't look good." Again a road on the far side suggests there may be a bridge. "Let's bushwhack downstream again and see if we get lucky."

But our progress grows increasingly difficult as the the bank becomes a field of boulders separated by the floodwaters. Venado lags behind while I push ahead, both of us watching the fast-flowing river, desperately searching for some sign—a bridge, or a fallen tree. But we see only the water's deep and violent insistence on going its own way.

Venado shouts, "Poppy!"

And I turn to see him pointing across the river; following the direction of his outstretched arm, I see two hikers on the opposite bank hunched over a map. Three other hikers in bright-colored rain jackets stand behind the first two and stare at us from under their hoods. Venado picks his way across the boulders and comes up next to me. He asks a question, but his child's voice gets lost in the din of the torrent and I cannot make it out.

We draw as near as we can to the bank, waving and hollering, until we get the attention of the hikers with the map. I sign with two downward fingers walking along my arm—a bridge—and point up and down the wild river.

The two hikers look at their map and start nodding. I turn smiling to Venado, but when I look back, one of them is shaking his head, pointing at the map, and the other nods in apparent agreement.

Raven Run

The one hollers through cupped hands. "You have to go back to the road! Go that way!" pointing back the way we'd come.

I call back. "No bridge?"

The others are certain: no bridge.

"What? What?" Venado is asking, as he's wont to do when he doesn't like what he's hearing.

"We have to go back to the road and hike around."

"Back?"

"I'm afraid so, my son."

We make our way back to the trail and Venado starts walking, and crying.

"Come here," I say, giving him a hug. "I'm crying too."

Once we get moving, accepting our fate, Venado resumes asking questions nonstop, and when we get close to the road, we see the red pickup truck coming back the other way. Running, we pop out of the woods just behind it yelling for our lives until it stops. We run down to the big machine as the window lowers on the passenger side.

The man and the young boy in the cab do not invite us soggy hikers in, but permit us to ride in the back. Venado tucks down out of the wind, sitting on a spare tire behind the cab.

We leave the muddy woods and drive a half a mile on a tarred road before the truck stops in front of a house. The driver climbs out and introduces himself: John Rinehart, the water manager for Hagerstown, Maryland. He controls the sluice gate for the big reservoir we can see in the distance behind his house. It becomes obvious to us: if we had followed Raven Run downstream, we would have ended up on a peninsula, looking across the water at a bridge we could not reach.

"Anything you guys need?" Rinehart asks, looking at the gaping holes in my poncho.

"Do you have an old rain jacket?" I ask. Rinehart goes into the house and returns with a heavy yellow raincoat, and a candy bar for Venado.

"How old are you?" Rinehart asks as Venado tears open his treat.

"Umm, seven," says Venado.

"Soon to be eight," I add, while tearing off the remnants of the Cambodian poncho and slipping into the comfort of the heavy jacket—wonderfully warm, windproof, and waterproof. A few minutes later, Rinehart drops us back on the trail on the opposite bank of Raven Run. We have backtracked two miles and hitched three to travel a hundred yards across that stream, and not a white blaze missed. Venado and I hump our wet gear up the steep trail out of the valley and hurry the last mile for Devils Racecourse, looking for a sign.

We come to a fork in the trail, and nailed high on a tree hangs a wet and battered strip of wood with "Devils Racecourse" carved in it. From there we follow a trail marked with blue blazes, back down, down—"Oh come on!" I say.

"Poppy, you're whining."

"Guilty. I'm the first to whine."

Down, down we go to the shelter, such as it is—three log walls chinked with white cement and capped with a crumpled tin roof, with a stream of runoff water flowing into the front opening. Quickening our pace, I call out, "Hello, the camp." We hear a whistle in response, and ducking under a tarp that covers the opening, we find a raised platform above the flooded ground. Two other hikers, a young woman and man wrapped up in fat purple sleeping bags, sit with their backs against the wall, riding out the storm.

"There's a leak there," says the young woman, pointing to a spot in the roof, above a puddle on the deck. "But you should be okay there," she adds, indicating a dry section.

While making quick introductions, Venado and I empty our packs and discover that everything except Venado's sleeping bag has gotten completely soaked. While the young man graciously boils water for our macaroni and cheese and tuna, we spread out our wet gear. Wolfing down our hot food, we share leftovers with our shelter mates, and after washing our bowls we squeeze into the one bag.

"Poppy?"

"Yeah?"

"You're squishing me."

"Yeah, it's tight; be glad we're small," I say, turning onto my side to create a bit more room in the bag.

Among other things, our first week on the trail proves to be a cold, wet exercise in adaptability, with a little help from friends.

"Why don't we carry a map?" Venado had asked on the retreat from Raven Run.

"Because other people do, and they always show up when you need them."

"Always?"

"Always. And if not, you figure something else out." I laugh, and then give him the simple truth. "We just can't carry everything we need. It's too much weight. We have to improvise as we go."

"What's improvise?"

What We're Getting Ourselves Into

If there's one thing that drives people to the extreme of thru-hiking the Appalachian Trail, it's desperation—in varying degrees. Ever since the first thru-hiker, Earl Shaffer, accomplished the feat in 1948 as a way to purge his psyche and soul after fighting in World War II, people have turned to the trail when they run out of options. Thru-hiking the AT gives them something to do, and it feels important.

For me, the time had come; as with Melville's Ishmael, "it was my substitute for pistol and ball." Stalled in my career, stalled in everything, I needed to find a place where my life had meaning. I had always shown my best out there in the wilds. I had the skills, or at least some of them; I could build a fire in the rain and had a good sense of direction and a clever mind. As a child, I had found my first escape route from the insanity called "civilization" in the forests of the East, and it felt right to share that with my son.

Venado, for his part, needed a break from a lifestyle that kept him between four walls and constrained his creativity. He was still a child—had yet to lose his first tooth—but in researching the trail we learned that a six-year-old had thru-hiked in 1980, and several eight-year-olds had gone the distance. I scoured the Internet to find a serious trekking pack for a sixty-pound boy and discovered the Tatonka Balloo. Venado's grandmother bought it for him, along with a green fleece pullover he wore every day. The pack came with a little stuffed buffalo hanging off the back, but Venado left that behind, because of the weight.

We were living and working in Mexico when we started making plans. "Do you know what you're getting into?" I had asked Venado. "No," he said.

But once out in the woods he skipped along as if liberated. When people asked if he missed home, and his mom, he would look at them funny. Of course he missed his mom, but not enough to surrender such abundant freedom. In the wide-open forest where everything he saw required examination, he scarcely noticed things like wet clothes and sore feet. The smells and textures, the wind and sounds all flooded his senses as the melting snow flooded the landscape, and to be there at an age when he still believed his father could do anything and always keep him safe meant he could suck it all up without a shred of anxiety to cloud his thinking.

I carried food and anxiety enough for both of us. I hit the trail broke and unemployed. I'd had a few big splashes as an environmental writer, but never achieved the notoriety of guys like Michael Pollan or even Bill McKibben. I had chased my passion through numerous countries, and it was exciting, but it didn't profit us monetarily; eventually my wife found work at home in Maine.

"You have to come back to the United States sometime," she told me.

"I'll be there to hike the trail with Venado," I told her.

The solid foundation we'd established in our relationship before children had grown pretty shaky in the last few years. We were making a valiant attempt to keep our kids' world and ours together, but our family had reached a point where the future dropped into an abyss that looked different for each of us. Being survivors, we came more or less to the same conclusion: We had to do something. Following Venado, with his unarticulated motives, we took on the Appalachian Trail. ■

2

THE BARBARIAN UTOPIA

"If these people were on the skyline, and kept their eyes open, they would see the things that the giant could see."

—Benton MacKaye, 1921

Venado and I wake up to more rain. Venado follows my lead as I put my bare feet into damp boots and leave the laces loose—drying them from the inside. Looking at all our soaked clothing and equipment draped around the shelter, we opt to stay put and make a fire. Building a fire in the rain takes patience, and our shelter mates watch from their bags as Venado and I snap pieces of dead wood off a laurel bush, split them, and shave off slivers of the inner wood until we have a a handful. "Standing dead wood always burns," I say.

Venado nods. "Yeah, I know that."

Venado shaves bits of magnesium from his fire starter into the pile of chips, and we wrap the tinder in some blank pages torn from one of our notebooks. I put this combustible bomb on a flat rock and cover it with a mound of the thinnest twigs we can find and a pile of thin damp wood on top of that.

"Once we get a good bed of coals going we'll be all set," I explain as I set the paper bundle alight. The first bundle burns out, but with careful attention on our second try we get the fire burning big and hot, and soon the raindrops land hissing on the stones around it.

All morning we change into our various damp clothes and stand steaming by the fire, making forays for more wood and chatting with our shelter mates, who we learn come from Philly. The guy, Chip, is a tall and skinny political activist/puppet maker; the woman, Shinara, sits against the wall of the shelter, with a knit hat over her long dark hair. "I work at a health food store on South Street," she tells us.

"Ah, South Street," I say. "Home of the not-so-healthy cheese steak."

"Poppy grew up there," Venado tells them.

"You're from Philly?" Chip asks.

"Near there."

"Where do you live now?"

"East Machias, Maine, and Mexico," says Venado.

"East Machias? Do you know . . ." Chip's been there and reels off the names of people we know in common, and we comment on the small-worldness of the trail.

Then come the other questions, inevitably. "Why are you out here? Whose idea was it?" Shinara wants to know.

"It was his idea," I tell them, nodding toward Venado, who squats in the mud and cant stop poking at the fire with a stick. He disputes my claim.

"No, yours," he says, turning his head quickly toward me.

"Mine?"

"Yeah, you said we could hike the trail."

"No, you asked if we could hike the trail, and I said, 'we can think about it,' and we did, and here we are."

"Yeah, but before that you said that me and you could hike the trail."

"*You and I,*" I correct him. "I was just telling you about it; you were the one who asked if we could actually go."

We decide to share the blame for having the idea, and while Venado sees things simply—we're here because we are here—I throw out a few plausible reasons: about wanting a good education for my children, about getting older and wanting to share something important with my son, about it being Venado's idea. They're all more-or-less true.

Out of politeness, Chip and Shinara accept the answers without digging into my dissembling. I turn the question back to them. What brought them out here?

They had planned to go to a spiritual retreat, they said, but it was expensive and they decided they could find just as much spirituality on the trail.

"That's what Benton MacKaye wanted," I say.

Chip and Shinara have not heard of MacKaye.

"MacKaye was the visionary of the AT," I tell them. "He said, 'the philosophy of through trails is to organize a Barbarian invasion, a countermovement to the metropolitan invasion of the wilderness.' He said, 'the Appalachian range needs to be put into public hands as the site for a Barbarian Utopia.'" I enunciate the words very clearly. It's a story Venado has already heard several times.

"MacKaye wasn't really a Barbarian in the wild sense," I tell Chip and Shinara. "He was more of a nineteenth-century Utopian stuck in a twentieth-century reality. Maybe he picked up the Barbarian thing from Teddy Roosevelt, who he worked for. Roosevelt said: 'Unless we keep the Barbarian virtues, gaining the civilized ones will be of little avail.' Or maybe Teddy got that from MacKaye. The idea is that people need to understand how natural systems work and make that the basis for development decisions. MacKaye said that in order to understand life people need connection to three critical things: community, rural processes, and wilderness. His vision of the trail provides all three to the urbanites, the 'civilizees' as he called them, who have become more and more disconnected from anything real."

I find myself giving a lecture, and the pair's attention ebbs and flows as they get up and pack to leave. But I can't stop pulling this philosophical metaphor of cultural survival over the various meltdowns that have backed my family to the wall, leaving the idea of the trail as the only option that makes sense.

"Once I read MacKaye's essay 'An Appalachian Trail' and his 'Barbarian Utopia' speech, that was it. I was totally hooked," I tell them. "MacKaye wanted to have communally owned camps at intervals along the trail—they'd be self-supporting through sustainable logging and farming. That's where you'd get the connection to community and rural processes, and then get in touch with wilderness by hiking between the camps. A lot of what we're planning to do is to try and find the places where MacKaye's vision is manifesting, intentionally or accidentally, and hopefully write about it."

Chip and Shinara have their bags packed, and they sit on the edge of the lean-to, enjoying the fire and looking out at the rain. The tree trunks stand naked and black, with low-hanging branches dripping from every elbow. On the wet ground every upturned leaf holds a little puddle of water, and runoff burbles steadily down the trail.

"This is our new home," says Venado, repeating a joke we have made up. "It has a leaky roof, a dirty floor, and the walls are very drafty, but it's big."

They laugh.

"How much longer you folks out for?" I ask.

"We were heading for Harpers Ferry," says Shinara. "But the rain."

"What'll you do now?"

She says their new plan is to hike to the road, hitch back to their car, and head home.

We say goodbye and watch them go. Venado returns to the fire.

"Try and stay clean," I tell him.

"Poppy?"

"Yes."

"Did Benton MacKaye invent the trail?"

"No, there were other trails; he just put the pieces together."

And Venado puts the pieces together by questioning and listening to me expound about MacKaye's vision to virtually anyone willing to listen.

I pull MacKaye's book *From Geography to Geotechnics* out of my pack and begin to read. "Sign the register, Venado, and then write in your journal." But he is out in the rain, busily building dams and dikes that channel the runoff away from the shelter.

The next morning, after bowls of granola soaked in powdered milk, we prepare to hit the trail in a fading drizzle, heading for Pennsylvania—the land where I was born.

"What do you think of when you think of a Barbarian?" I ask Venado.

"Um, a Native American?"

"That's kind of a stereotype. I think MacKaye meant it as anyone who knows that water flows downhill, and that the sun lifts water uphill."

"The sun lifts water?"

"Yeah, the sun heats water, evaporation makes clouds, clouds rain on mountains, voila! It's working all the time."

Venado takes that one in. "But what's utopia?" he asks.

"According to MacKaye, it's a pipe dream. There's two kinds: One is the utopia of making your pipe dream come true, like us here on the trail—for most people this is unimaginable. The other is to go to the movies and identify with the characters who make their pipe dreams come true. What do you prefer, hiking the trail or watching movies?"

"I like both."

"Me too. But this hike is real, and the movie is not. MacKaye said there are two kinds of utopias: one of creative action, and the other of effortless escape. I think Barbarians choose creative action."

Back in Mexico, Venado had witnessed me lobbying his mother to support the hike. He might not have been able to articulate it, but even at his age he would have felt the unbearable tension undermining our family. It manifested as a scarcity of smiles.

"Listen to this, listen," I had said to my wife, reading from a handful of papers that still smelled of the printer. "'The problem of living is at bottom an economic one. And this alone is bad enough, even in a period of so-called "normalcy." But living has been considerably complicated of late in various ways—by war, by questions of personal liberty, and by "menaces" of one kind or another. There have been created bitter antagonisms. We are undergoing also the bad combination of high prices and unemployment. This situation is world wide—the result of a world-wide war.' MacKaye wrote that in 1921. You'd have thought he wrote it last week. He started talking about this just a few months after his wife committed suicide; he saw the trail as a healing thing, in all kinds of ways."

Venado's mother had understood, but not agreed. "But why go now?" she'd asked.

"Look, I'm fifty-two. I have friends who get cancer and are gone in six months. This feels right; it's the right time. This is something he and I need. We all need it." I'd composed a rationale for her, but in fact, we had to go—were already gone—and she knew it.

"But we can't afford it."

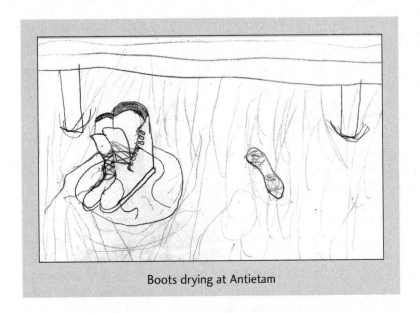

Boots drying at Antietam

"Even if we go into debt, it might be worth it. Besides, what would any of us have given at seven years old to ask for this and have the answer be yes?"

She'd reluctantly agreed. "I'll send food boxes for two months; after that, no promises."

"I'll be happy if we make two weeks," I say to Venado as we hike out from Devils Racecourse. But every day the sounds of our own footsteps—in mud, on rock, slapping through wet leaves—grow more familiar. Our packs mold to our backs, and calluses take the places of blisters. We stride along the ridge tops, looking out through the bare trees at the valleys below, "seeing what the giant could see," as MacKaye said, and in the afternoon of our seventh day we cross the Pennsylvania line and reach Deer Lick Shelter, a ten-mile hike from Devils Racecourse.

I head for the spring to get water. "I'll be right back," I tell Venado. "Wait here."

But he does not want to wait alone at the shelter and follows me to the spring.

Back at the shelter we are slow to unpack; someone has trashed the place, leaving open cans of food in the wet ashes of the fire pit and graffiti on the walls. Two strong-looking middle-aged women and a dog come by; without shedding their packs, they quickly sign the register and turn toward the trail again.

"How far you going?" I ask.

"Antietam or Tumbling Run," the smaller of the two says over her shoulder.

"Where'd you start?"

"Ensign Cowall. We do seventeen miles a day, every day."

And they're gone.

"What do you think, Venado? Should we go to Antietam? It's only three more miles."

"Okay, let's go."

And we take off following the recognizably small tracks of the women and their dog; they had signed the register "Two Hags and a Hound" and drawn a little picture of their dog. An hour and a half later we reach Antietam Creek. The water is still high, forcing us to pole-vault off the end of a bridge to reach the island where the shelter stands.

"I guess they must've gone on," I say, looking into the empty lean-to. "Imagine if we were down in Georgia with the crowd. The shelters would all be full and we'd be pitching our tent."

"Poppy?"

"Yeah?"

"Can the water come up here?" Venado is looking at the matted grass around the shelter.

"It can. But I think it's going down." I point to the creek, mispronouncing the name "Antietam" like it almost rhymes with "Vietnam." "This flows down into Maryland and through one of the bloodiest battlegrounds of the Civil War. Something like twenty thousand dead and wounded in a day. I don't know."

"We cross a Civil War battlefield every day," Venado says later, staring into a fire he has built with some guidance.

"Yeah, some I didn't even know about. We're almost past them all now. One more big one."

After a while we lie down with the firelight playing on the shelter walls and our still-damp clothing hanging all around us. Venado listens as I tell the story, again, of how our ancestor James Crader fought with the 153rd Pennsylvania Volunteers at Chancellorsville, the battle where the great Confederate general Stonewall Jackson was shot down by his own men.

"These stories came straight from my great-grandmother," I tell Venado. "James Crader was her father. Right after Chancellorsville, he fought at Gettysburg. His regiment got slammed and chased off Barlow's Knoll on the first day. But on the second day the Louisiana Tigers attacked them on Cemetery Ridge, and they held them off. He was only a corporal, but he commanded his company because all the officers above him got killed, and that's where he got wounded too, but not badly." In the faint light I can see Venado's eyes; they're open, and he's listening.

"He got discharged after that battle, but reenlisted with his father in the 47th Regiment and fought down south the rest of the war. His father died down there of dysentery and is buried in Natchez, Mississippi. Can you imagine reenlisting to go back into that nightmare? Cannonballs and bodies ripped to pieces and smoke and blood. I can only wonder what kind of man he was."

Venado apparently does not yet grasp the whole picture. "Was he a Confederate?"

"Oh, nonono. He was with the Pennsylvanians, in the Union Army, also called the Federals, or the Yankees. Funny thing is, there is a statue of American soldiers in Allentown, where he lived, and he was the model for the Confederate soldier."

There's so much to tell. I work around the edges of the bigger story, how Lee got drawn into the fight at Gettysburg, and what the loss of Jackson must have meant to him.

"Who won the Civil War?" Venado asks.

"Hard to say. Everybody loses something in war. But the Confederates surrendered in the end."

"Who were the Confederates?"

"That's a good question. The Confederates were the southern states that wanted to leave the Union and have their own country because the

North was giving them a hard time with taxes. And some of them wanted to have slaves, which most northerners didn't like. The North couldn't accept slavery."

"No."

"Right. Everyone needs to be free. Okay, let's see if we can name the Confederate states. Wanna start?"

And we name them, near as we can, working out the list together: Florida, Georgia, South Carolina, North Carolina, Virginia—but not West Virginia—Tennessee, Alabama, Mississippi, Louisiana, Texas. "That's ten," I say. "But I think there're thirteen stars on the Confederate flag. We'll have to look it up. Arkansas? Missouri? Kentucky maybe." The conversation peters out and we fall asleep.

Climbing back up to the ridgeline under clear skies the next morning, we stop and talk to a logger cutting down a grove of chestnut oaks. Standing by a fresh-felled tree, the tip of his long chainsaw poking into a pile of wood chips on the ground, the man in greasy orange leggings—safety chaps—tips his hard hat back and explains in an almost southern accent how a few years before a gypsy moth infestation had wiped out the oaks on this mountain.

"What are gypsy moths?" Venado wants to know.

"It's a worm that eats the leaves off the trees," the logger says.

A few miles on, we enter Caledonia State Park and look out through the leafless trees onto wide valleys of seemingly untouched woods. It goes on all day, with barely a sign of human activity. At Chimney Rocks we take a play break, threading through the caves and tunnels formed by a glacial tumble of rocks, and then we march on.

Eight days into the trail, and four days after leaving the cleanliness of the Free State Hikers Hostel, Venado breaks out of the trees above a highway thirteen miles west of Gettysburg. A layer of soot from the fire pits dulls the flower print design on his once bright orange pack. Dirty, with long, uncombed hair, he looks a bit rough, like a Confederate boy soldier marching out of the south.

Looking just as grimy and sporting a week-old beard, I follow him onto the cleared slope above the road. We scrabble down the naked hill to the smooth, white-lined asphalt and stand there for a minute, stunned by exhaust fumes from trucks and traffic streaming by.

"Good lord."

"Poppy, people think Barbarians are stinky, but these civilizees really stink."

"Oh man, if anybody complains about the way we smell, we'll just tell 'em to go stick their nose up their exhaust pipe. Wow—it's hard to imagine that we wallow in this filth and hardly know it."

Walking along the road, I pick up an open Wi-Fi signal with my iPhone and make a Skype call home. After a brief conversation I pass the phone to Venado. "Here, say hi to your mom." And the boy chatters away to his mother and sister until I cut him off.

"Come on. We've gotta go."

Creative Action

When asked why we had come out to the trail, I might also have mentioned this truth: "Children come into the world knowing what they need and how to get it, and this is a case in point. We are out here to save our family from destruction; Venado knew that intuitively, and that's why he asked to go."

What had cinched the deal, compelling us to walk the two thousand–mile spine of the Appalachians, was stumbling across the essays of Benton MacKaye, the visionary of the Appalachian Trail. MacKaye broached the idea in 1921, a few months after his wife jumped into New York's East River and drowned herself. The trail through the wilderness originated as the product of his personal despair and expanded into a refuge from an increasingly confused and confusing civilization.

Modern humans—bombarded with radiation from cell phones, iPods, and all of what Venado called "electronic world-destroyer devices"—could catch a breath in this place that, if you paid attention and used your imagination, could feel primal.

Our early days on the trail proved to be the most challenging, but also the most blessed. Every day we stayed out there seemed like a victory, every mile a major accomplishment.

Triumphal, we crossed into Pennsylvania, a mere forty miles from our starting point. Fueled by the epiphanies that MacKaye's essays kindled, we marched on in search of his utopia, or at least some signs of its passing.

The hike itself had actually been inspired by a movie we rented in Mexico, *El Último Mohicano—The Last of the Mohicans,* the story of Chingachgook and his son Uncas, the last of the Mohicans, fighting in 1757 in the French and Indian War. Venado took his name, "the deer," from the son, Uncas, whose name in French was *le cerf agile*—"the swift deer." Chingachgook meant "big snake," which didn't appeal to me, so I took my name from the Mexican slang for "owl." I heard later that it also meant "watchman" or "guard," which seemed appropriate. Bearing Spanish monikers derived from Native Americans, we played at being back in early America, back in the world where our Mohawk, Dutch, and French ancestors roamed the woods of the north. Walking through the empty forests, we projected ourselves into a primeval illusion that, in our early days on the trail, kept us going.

I hadn't spent much time in the woods with my own father, but I'd learned about creative action from him. Every Saturday from the time he could hold a bat until he tore a tendon at age seventy-three, he was on the diamond or gridiron, playing baseball or football with his pals—for fun.

"He even played the day I was born," I told Venado, who expressed surprise.

"On your birthday?"

"It was a Saturday," I shrugged, and laughed. "They called him 'Charlie Brown' because he did all the organizing."

Unlike some sports fanatics (the word "fan" is derived from "fanatic") who project themselves so thoroughly into their teams and heroes that they unleash destructive orgies over victory or defeat, my father and his friends got off the couch and onto the field. At the end of most games they would come back to the house and, over a few beers, rehash their *own* triumphs and defeats.

MacKaye saw the Appalachian Trail as a place for spiritual awakening that began with a physical, confidence-building experience. He envisioned urban workers, with a need to triumph in some way, walking up to the top of a mountain and seeing the world at their feet. They could be giants.

The idea is to climb to the ridgeline through one's own effort, to *become* a giant. ■

3

TRAVELING LIGHT: AN AT EDUCATION

"Never let school get in the way of your education."
—Mark Twain

"What about school?" asks an out-of-work teacher we meet on the trail.

"I'm homeschooled," Venado tells him.

"Hiking the AT is an education for grown-ups, let alone an eight-year-old," I say to the teacher. He tells us his name is Jeff, and we introduce ourselves and talk a bit. At the end of our brief conversation I ask how far to the shelter.

"Not far at all," he tells us. "Less than an hour."

But along the way we stop to examine our first rhododendron thicket. "It's like mangroves," says Venado, looking around in wonder. Stopping frequently to admire the scenery and take pictures, we take well over an hour to reach the well-kept and beautiful Quarry Gap Shelter. The logs that make up its walls are straight and well chinked with white cement—everything swept and neat.

The next morning, March 17, St. Patrick's Day, we wake up just the two of us.

"Happy birthday, Venado."

We celebrate his eighth birthday by putting in our longest day yet, fifteen miles of questions, which we often answer together. "Is there anyplace on earth where there is no life?" Venado asks.

We work on that, wondering about the south pole, the top of Mount Everest, and the deepest oceans. "I suppose that even in those places there's some bacteria or something."

"Well really the whole earth is alive, so there can't be anyplace that's not alive," say Venado.

"Exactly."

He asks if people could ever be one big family. "We *are* one big family," I tell him. "The question is, will people ever realize it?"

He goes on, telling me that all humans are descended from Native Americans, and I suggest that we're all descended from native people: Native Europeans, Native Africans, and so on, and we arrive toward dusk at Toms Run Shelters, a nondescript place with two separate shelters and a water source that does not inspire confidence. "We'll change it out as soon as we find a nice spring," I say to Venado after filling our bottles from a runoff-flooded pool downhill from the privy.

Two hikers from Georgia, an uncle and his nephew, occupy one of the shelters, and Venado and I take the other. The Georgians share their fire and a weather report. "Supposed to go down to twenty-seven," says the uncle. He is just back from military service in Afghanistan and he shows Venado a gurkha blade, a wicked-looking curved knife.

As darkness falls and the temperature drops, Venado and I zip our sleeping bags together and crawl in for the night. Long after the fire has died, Venado rouses and starts to crawl out of the bag. I grab his arm. "Where're you going? Are you going to pee?" He grumbles as he shakes loose and disappears into the moonless night. I fall back asleep, waking a while later when Venado comes back.

"Brrrr," he says, crawling into our sleeping bag.

"Where were you? Did you go pee?"

Again he mumbles an incoherent response and we both fall back asleep.

Next morning we rise at first light and hit the trail, intending to warm up a bit before eating breakfast. Hiking along, I ask Venado about why he got up in the night, but he has no recollection of getting up. I tell him what happened and he says he does not remember any of it.

Fire at Toms Run

"Were you dreaming?"

"I did have a dream. It was really funny."

"What was it?"

"Kittens in a garbage can, and there was a jumping mouse rolling a rock away from its door, and the rock rolled into the wheel of a car going by and bounced off, and then somebody picked it up and it turned to dust."

"What happened with the kittens?"

"I don't know. That's all I remember."

"So what was funny?

"It was funny when it turned to dust."

"I've been having weird dreams too," I tell him and describe climbing down the framework on the inside of a hotel, and I can't find room number 1029, and I'm visiting Justin Cronin, a writer whose apartment is full of piled-up furniture, and he invites me to sit down, but there is nowhere to sit. "And then I looked into a mirror and I was tall and wearing a red wig, and when I took it off my hair was blond."

"Poppy, that is weird."

"I told you it was."

Later, we begin reciting the names of all the shelters we've stayed at:.

"Ed Garvey, Rocky Run, Pogo Campground, Free State Hikers Hostel, Devils Racecourse, Devils Racecourse"—we say it twice because we stayed there two nights.

"Antietam, Quarry Gap, and Toms Run," finishes Venado.

"That's a good memory exercise. I wonder if we can do it all the way to Katahdin."

"That'll be a lot of names," Venado says, sounding a little daunted.

We follow the trail down into Pine Grove Furnace, the remains of an ironworks similar to many others that once played an important role in Pennsylvania's economy.

At a picnic table I try to light our alcohol stove, but my lighter fails many times before it makes a flame. Once the little brass stove gets going I heat a pot of powdered milk on it and pour the thin mix onto our granola. Venado draws water from an outdoor faucet, but even when he lets it run for ten minutes it still tastes like rust—so we put orange-flavored powdered drink mix in it.

While eating we wander around the stone furnace that stands two stories high, tapering like an unfinished pyramid. We study placards with old pictures showing what the furnace looked like in operation: crowds of men, teams of horses, mountains of charcoal and lime, and a big white wooden building extending out over the furnace from a low hill, all caught in sepia stillness. Venado reads the accompanying text and struggles to make sense of the iron-making process. I realize the prose of the placards leaves a bit to be desired, but reading together we get the gist of it.

"It looks like they piled layers of lime, charcoal, and ore in the furnace, lit it, and then forced air in so that the charcoal burned extra hot," I say. "Apparently the whole works turned into a slurry of molten mess and the iron sank to the bottom."

"How did they get it out?"

"Says they opened those gates and it flowed out into molds called pigs. So this must be pig iron, just like in the Johnny Cash song 'Rock Island Line': 'I got pig iron, I got pig iron.' They must've dumped all the stuff in from that building."

"You can see where it was," says Venado, pointing to a stone foundation on the hill behind the furnace.

Further on we pass the halfway mark for those who started hiking on Springer Mountain. "Our halfway mark will be down in Virginia somewhere," I tell Venado.

Walking dirt roads the miles fly by. We pass camps, and a house with a driveway marked "This is NOT the trail." At Birch Run Shelters we meet a woman with a daypack and she asks Venado if he and I are out for the night.

"Yes," he tells her.

"Say, you don't have any matches or a lighter do you?" I ask. "Our lighter is running out of fuel."

"Not with me."

A tall thin guy hiking with one pole comes into view, strolling toward the shelter.

"We met that guy a couple of days ago," says Venado. "I remember the way he walks. That's Jeff."

"Yeah," I say, smiling. "That's Jeff, the biology teacher. He must spend a lot of time out here." I hit the familiar hiker up for a lighter as soon as he reaches the shelter.

"I don't know what I've got in here," Jeff says, rummaging through his daypack—to no avail. "Up at the car."

We sit around the picnic table talking, and Jeff and the woman get onto the subject of hemlocks, something wrong with the hemlocks. Venado and I hear the word *adelgid* for the first time. "What is it?"

"The hemlock woolly adelgid," says Jeff. "It's a true bug that's infecting the hemlocks, killing them." He looks around and spots a hemlock. "I'll bet there's some there."

We all follow him over to the tree and he lifts the tip of a low branch. "There they are," he says and points to tiny white fluff balls, snowflakes tucked in around some of the needles.

"What's it called again?"

"The hemlock woolly adelgid. It came over in a packing crate from China and has been spreading up and down the Appalachian Mountains. The hemlock is the state tree of Pennsylvania, but in twenty years there won't be any more here."

"Oh man."

"The only thing that makes me feel good," says Jeff, "is that I heard they have just as much trouble with our bugs killing their trees over there."

Venado and I exchange curious glances at this remark.

The woman heads back to her car, and Jeff, who had been heading south, decides to turn around and hike north with us. A half a mile from the shelter we see a group of shirtless, thuggish-looking guys coming towards us. One is looking straight at me.

"Do you need a lighter?"

"What?"

"We heard you needed a lighter."

"Yeah."

He gives me a lighter.

"Thanks."

He waves. "No problem."

At the parking lot the woman has found another lighter in her car and offers it to us, but we decline.

Jeff finds a lighter in his car and insists Venado take it, "as a backup."

We hike on with Jeff as our guide. He shows us how to identify the pitch pine—two needles, twisted.

Venado asks about gypsy moths and Jeff explains the insect's morphology; he shows us how to spot empty egg casings in the furrows of the bark of the chestnut oaks.

"Luckily we're having a wet spring, and we had a cold wet spring last year so most of the eggs died before they hatched," says Jeff. "They don't like a lot of rain."

"Is it an invasive species?" Venado asks.

"Yes, they brought them here in the eighteen hundreds to make silk."

Around 1868, Etienne Leopold Trouvelot, an amateur entomologist with an interest in silkworms, had brought gypsy moth egg cases from France to Medford, Massachusetts, where the larvae escaped. Since then, gypsy moth outbreaks have plagued the eastern forests. Two major outbreaks in Pennsylvania in 1978 and 1986 cost the state over two hundred million dollars in lost timber.

Of course you could say that we descendents of Europeans are an invasive species in North America. Or you could say that we're all travelers on this planet. If the option presents itself, we exploit new opportunities.

It boils down to perspective. Like when my daughter asked once if we were lost. "Of course we're lost," I told her. "We're all stuck on this big molten rock flying through space and no one has a clue where we are."

Jeff leads us through the woods until we come into a scattering of black locust trees. "I want to show you something," he says. "Come on over here." He steps off the trail and waves us over to a mound of dirt. "These are Allegheny mound ants."

Venado squats down to examine the hill with brown and black ants pouring all over it, while Jeff explains how to identify them—first two parts of the body are brown, the last part black. He explains how they have a matrilineal succession—queen to queen to queen—and how colonies will accept workers from other colonies.

"All this dirt comes from their tunnels, Venado, so you can imagine this ground here is laced with tunnels."

"Why do they live near the black locust?"

"That's a good question. They have a relationship with the black locusts because these ants actually farm other bugs on the locust. There's this bug, the thorn mimic bug, that lives on the locust and looks like one of its thorns. They make a sugar that the ants collect, and the ants protect them."

"How do they protect them?" Venado asks.

"Well, they don't let any other bugs on the tree. Once, as an experiment, I threw a beetle on there, and they went crazy."

"Did they kill it?"

"No, they just kicked it off. But it was a Japanese beetle, so no love lost."

We continue walking, often stopping to examine more ant mounds. It's a bright warm day and at one point Venado goes lightly up the trail.

"Hey Venado? Where's your pack?"

"Oh!"

Jeff and I wait while Venado runs back to retrieve his pack.

As we trek on I explain our plan to Jeff. It's an anti–Lyme disease hike. We intend to head north from Harpers Ferry to Vermont in March and April, to get through the worst Lyme disease areas before the ticks that carry the bacterial disease come out too thick. Then we will take the train south to Springer Mountain, Georgia, and hike north again to Harpers Ferry, then jump back to Vermont and on to Mt. Katahdin in Maine, the trail's end—and home. Jeff nods in approval and shares some of what he knows about the Smoky Mountains in North Carolina. "I used to work down there. I'm actually a forester. When you get down there you'll be hiking through the balds, and if you get there at the right time, when the azaleas bloom, you'll see a spectacular sight."

"What are the balds?"

"They're these big open areas on the tops of the mountains."

"Above the tree line?"

"No, there's no tree line down there, just these big natural meadows. Or they used to be natural. Our job was to cut down the trees and shrubs to keep them open. Used to be farmers would graze their cattle up there, and before that, the Indians would burn them. But they believe that originally they were created by megafauna, giant sloths and woolly mammoths."

I ask about the weather down south, the terrain, the water, and Jeff proves to be a veritable treasure trove of solid information. I tell him about how Benton MacKaye had proposed that fourteen nature guide centers be established along the trail, and how people would be able to walk with informed guides and develop an understanding of, and connection with, the flora and fauna of the various sections of the trail. "That's what you're doing," I tell Jeff. "Maybe when we establish the Barbarian Utopia, you can get paid for it."

The best lessons along the trail occur spontaneously, like Jeff deciding to turn around and hike north with a curious little boy. Or Venado picking up a hickory nut shell, floating it in a puddle and asking how boats sink, giving me a chance to explain the Archimedes principle.

One morning, walking ahead as he often does, Venado spots an albino squirrel. "A white squirrel!"

Pure white, it bounds across the forest floor and spirals around the back of a tree. We flank it so it must come into view for one of us but it keeps climbing, jumps to another tree, and escapes our probing gaze. Later, I talk about genetics, without getting too deep.

But when I try some formal education, it backfires. Venado resists having to calculate the mileage.

"What do I do?"

"You just get our beginning mile and our finishing mile from the guidebook, then subtract the lower number from the higher number."

"But what do you mean, subtract?"

"Are you serious, Venado? What's subtraction? You knew that last year. Come on, I'm going to get in a lot of trouble if I bring you home knowing less math than when you left."

"But I don't know what subtraction is," he says, watching me fume.

Toward the end of the day the trail winds through a rock maze, almost as if the trail maintainers wanted to play with us. But regardless of all the stops we have made with Jeff, we log our longest day yet, nineteen plus miles, and arrive at Alex Kennedy Shelter with daylight to spare. The next morning we have only four miles to go to Boiling Springs, and with time to kill, I insist that Venado draw some pictures and write in his journal. But somewhere back on the trail I had shown him how to make a pretend pipe from an acorn and a stick, and Venado concentrates on scraping out the insides of an acorn.

"Come on, Venado, put that away."

Walking around camp with a newly made pipe clenched in his teeth like Huck Finn, Venado puts up a fight. "What do you want me to write?"

"Anything, write about what you've seen."

"But I can't think of anything."

"Draw a picture then."

"Of what?"

"Anything!"

"Why did you get yellow paper?"

My jaw bulges as the muscles tighten. This is where it gets hard: resistance.

Jeff might have known how to cope with resistance in students, but he left Venado and me the previous afternoon at a fork in the trail that looped around back to his car. Walking on, passing plants and insects we know nothing about, we miss his company. Venado and I have to figure out the schooling, and nature, on our own, and while I might admit that my little boy's learning works best when self-directed, I refuse to surrender the homeschooling agenda. Venado, for his part, shows no signs of buying in—he's free now.

Our Manifesto!

Before we left Mexico, I jumped out of bed very early one morning and ran barefoot out to the thatch-roofed bungalow where I worked. I sat down at the computer, roosters crowing, dogs barking in the background, and wrote a stream-of-consciousness manifesto:

"The Temporary Conquest"
and so . . .

There is the temporary conquest of the mind, the compulsion to create order, to control thought. In the mind a hierarchy becomes organized, prioritizing what is seen, heard. All senses come to being within the system. What is outside is the wasteland of the mind, where banished thoughts howl.

And such is Empire, it cannot stand, it cannot hold back the Barbarians at the gates. They are too many.

This is why we are leaving now, my son and I, to go off into the mountains and walk in the forests for days on end, to watch spring come and feel its warmth, to howl in the wilderness and remember possibilities.

This is what I believe Benton MacKaye meant when he said the long trail was "meant to organize a Barbarian invasion." He was intending to create a physical expression of what happens in the mind, what it longs for, and doesn't know: freedom from the fascism of organized thought. Logic is useless. The conquest cannot stand, it never could.

I see the sparkle of human energy melding and blending the black and white energies running in straight lines shot through by the color and burst of the Barbarian thoughts.

What MacKaye wanted to do was to raise consciousness, to open the gates and let the Barbarians in, to welcome them and all their "cleansing influence," as he called it.

The same cleansing one feels in escaping from the crush and demands of a regimented consciousness. To go into the woods and permit oneself to breathe and listen to what has not been deemed important.

All of this hierarchy is inflicted, you see. It's a sickness of the imagination. And I am raging at it.

The Barbaric thoughts insist on entry, they scale the walls, more defenses are added, they never cease trying, and the conquered mind becomes a fortress, defending a smaller and smaller region of order.

This is what happens more and more in our minds. It is the method by which we are controlled. Our minds have shrunk to little pea brains wrapped around the myth of security, and order. The state promises to defend us, to control what enters our worlds. The state establishes borders to separate us, and at the border is where purity of thought is tested, where one can be probed and tested to be sure the infection is complete.

The mind's power to create must be controlled, we learn this without knowing—this message is inflicted on us.

I cannot say I will continue to go on as I have after I make this journey, and if I survive it—for sure it would be a good place to die, in the woods, to be consumed by maggots and beetles. My thoughts free at last.

In the waking thoughts, the voices of the Barbarians become comprehensible. They call from the wild and untamed regions of the mind, and vanish among the trees as the light of day strengthens. This is why it is good to be awake at dawn, and listening.

Eventually the conquest must fail, must fail in order for humans to evolve, this is true creative destruction, it is not so much physical, although the architecture too must change, it will follow the changing awareness of human beings. Some will grow faster than others, I saw this.

They may fall under the weight of the unawakened majority, but eventually enough will raise awareness.

This is like the stampeding buffaloes, never do they all run off the cliff, eventually they figure it out. The awareness grows.

When the Barbaric thoughts come, I want to welcome them without fear. The civilized mind is cursed this way. It wants to cage the wild, appreciate it from a separate space, control its influences, but the power of nature never ceases to humble us. It is the Barbarian, and in our refusal to accept its realities, the life and death of it, we condemn ourselves to suffering, fear, and rage.

So in the Barbarian Utopia, we complete this piece of ourselves. We can move on, mentally stable in the midst of limitless thought, accepting that it will offer what we need, when we need it.

This is for me the ultimate returning. This is where I was born, and where I first knew who I was. Pennsylvania, where I first knew myself as man, as being, and understood what I could not say, and felt myself cursed with this awareness.

I will remember the stories of our time before, when all the world spoke to us and we knew how to listen. And our ancestors, whom we hear in the wind, will protect and guide us. We will do this. ∎

4

ROCKS

On the way in to Boiling Springs we cross a bridge over a stream so clear we can see the orange rocks of its bed. Trout fishermen, all in high rubber boots or chest waders, stand in the shallows of the fast-flowing water. Gracefully, they whip long streamers of line from their fly rods and settle their lures near the deep pools. The trail leads into the heart of the little village, and after picking up a small resupply box at the post office, we sort out our gear at a picnic table in front of the Appalachian Trail Conservancy's Mid-Atlantic Regional Office. Venado spots a groundhog. Wildlife! He directs my eye to it, and we watch it rooting around near the stream that bubbles up from the spring that gives the town its name.

Leaving our packs at the Appalachian Trail Conservancy office we head off to indulge in a proper celebration of Venado's birthday, complete with Pennsylvania food: TastyKakes and hoagies. It's the first really warm day we've had, and after our meal we sit barefoot in the grass behind a community building, letting the sun warm our dumpling-white feet. Examining my two-hundred-dollar boots I make the sickening discovery that they have opened a seam. Boots are everything on the trail, and I spend an hour negotiating with REI about a replacement pair—not that REI isn't helpful, only that the Wi-Fi signal I am borrowing keeps fading out and dropping my Skype call. "Hi, this is the guy you were just talking to . . . "

Venado's sixty-dollar L.L. Bean boots are doing fine, but right now the grass is tickling his toes as he explores around the closed rec center. He runs over to where I sit with pen and paper, iPhone clamped between my shoulder and ear. "Excuse me, what did you say? The connection here is not so good."

"Poppy, I have to go poop."

I look at him and point to the woods. He turns and frowns at the scrubby lowland forest.

"Poppy, I have to go. Is there a bathroom here?"

I give him a stern look and point to the woods. "Ah, phooey." I look at the phone and start to redial. "You're on your own, Venado. I gotta take care of this."

Around noon we return to the ATC office and wait for our couch-surfing host to come pick us up. The year before, I had chanced upon a website, www.couchsurfing.org, and joined what billed itself as "a trust-building movement." The way it worked, you offered your couch to travelers in need of a place to stay, and other members offered you their couches when you needed a place to stay—simple enough.

Our host is Adam Weber, from nearby Mechanicsburg, "the only northern city ever occupied by the Confederate Army during the Civil War," he tells us on the way to his house, an old brick federal-style building owned by his parents and divided into four apartments. "During the Battle of Gettysburg, they just marched in and took over."

Our invasion is much more chill. Adam has piles of interesting books he's reading, but it's a cartoon book we find in his bathroom, *Unpleasant Ways to Die,* that Venado and I cannot get enough of. We laugh hysterically at a drawing of a mountain climber roped to another who is falling past him, another of a baby's feet sticking out from under a pile of cans in a grocery cart, the mother screaming.

After Venado and I take baths and get our laundry done, the three of us stroll down the quiet tree-lined street to a cafe, passing a hardware store that Adam's grandfather had owned. Over burgers, Venado explains the hike to Adam and answers all his questions while I alternate between watching people in the cafe and working on the Internet. "Are you finding what you're looking for?" Adam asks, distracting me from distraction.

I snap back to the present and nod. "Yeah, yeah, we're going to stop at this place called the Creekside Cultural Center. It sounds a lot like the kind of communal camp MacKaye wanted to establish, and it's right near the trail."

Adam drops us back in Boiling Springs the next morning, and before heading into the woods we buy an emergency water filter for ten dollars at an outdoors store. "I get more skeptical about the water down here on the flats with all these farms," I tell Venado. I tuck the filter into my pack and we head off for Darlington Shelter, where I had stayed on New Year's Eve 1975.

The day begins with us hiking through people's backyards, then we pass a shooting range that sounds like armageddon, and cross bridges over roaring highways. I mention that this is the last day of winter, and that tonight is the vernal equinox.

"Poppy, what is the vernal equinox?"

"It's when the day is twelve hours long everywhere on the planet. The earth is passing the point where we begin spring and people in the southern hemisphere are beginning fall."

Skirting farmers' fields we meet a middle-aged couple and mention that this is the day of the vernal equinox. "Is that so?" says the woman.

"The day will be twelve hours long everywhere in the world," Venado tells her.

"Is that so?" she says glancing over at me. I nod in confirmation. "I never knew that," she says, looking at her husband. "Did you know that?"

He shrugs. They laugh and we part company.

"Poppy? How could she not know that?" Venado asks, further on.

"Different people know different things," I tell him. "Everybody can learn from everybody else."

Mid-afternoon, we stop at an old farm to eat a late lunch and fill up on water. Sitting at a picnic table set up under the overhang of a stone barn painted stucco-white, like the nearby house, I draw Venado's attention to the style of the place. "This is like my grandparents' farm."

A man sporting a thin gray beard comes over to talk to us, and we quickly slip into an easy rapport, like old friends. His name is Bruce, and the idea of an eight-year-old intending to hike the entire trail intrigues him.

"You're welcome to stay here," he says. "We're having a party and there'll be about twenty kids here."

Venado grabs hold of the idea. "Poppy, we were going to hike fourteen miles today and ten tomorrow—why don't we just hike ten today and fourteen tomorrow?"

"I can tell you too that there's a troop of boy scouts up at Darlington for the night," says Bruce, and the idea of a crowded shelter ahead convinces us to stay put.

Venado and I throw our gear into an unused bunk room behind the main house and settle in to celebrate the vernal equinox.

The kids play croquet. I meet people who know people I went to high school with. In Pennsylvania, many meetings are one degree of separation for an old Keystone kid like me. And in the morning, Michele Landis, the boss of the house, makes it clear: "You guys are not leaving here without a breakfast."

Pancakes, bacon, eggs, fruit, toast, coffee—it all goes down fast, while Bruce entertains us by trying to balance an egg on its end. "Supposedly this can only be done on the equinox," he says. But he has to seat it in the dimpled end of a cantaloupe to make it work. "There," he says, and we applaud. We make a late departure, covering trail I have not seen in thirty-five years.

"I remember this, I remember it," I keep saying as we make our way up toward Darlington.

"Tell me when we get to the place where you killed the rattlesnake, Poppy."

"Okay."

"How did you kill it?"

"It was on the trail, stretched out, and I was just about to step on it when I saw it, and I jumped over it. My heart was beating *baboom baboom*, and then it coiled up and started to rattle, so I just grabbed a rock and smashed it. I did it a couple of times because I wanted to be very sure it was dead."

"What if it bit you?" Venado wants to know, and he turns to look at me.

"Watch where you're going. I'd probably be dead, because all I had on were sneakers and a pair of shorts. I had already made camp at the shelter."

We stop for lunch at Darlington—no sign of the boy scouts. A young couple and an older man appear, wandering around silently, looking like they had just buried a body or something. We watch them from a distance. "Maybe they're mushroom hunters, or looking for a lost treasure"—but we don't ask.

"Okay," I say as we pack up after lunch. "Ten miles, mostly a ridge walk, so let's do it."

We stride along, heading for Cove Mountain.

"Poppy?"

"Yes?"

"Are we going to stay in a shelter, or go to the Doyle?"

"Depends," I say, citing the variables. "If there's good water at the shelter, we should stay there. We don't have money to spend on many hotels."

"Was the trail here when you were little?" Venado asks as we walk along.

"Oh yeah. It's been here since nineteen thirty-seven, or thirty-nine, I can't remember. But back then it was a lot of road walking. We're keeping to the woods a lot more than when I was here before."

"How did you find out about it?"

"Up at the farm, my grandfather and Uncle Donald were talking about the Horseshoe Trail, how it went near the farm and all the way to the Appalachian Trail. And I asked about it. Like you, I was a man of many questions."

"What did they say?"

"They told me it was a trail that went all the way from Georgia to Maine, but your sense of geography is better than mine was at the time, and I didn't get it. I sure wouldn't have imagined walking it."

It's a warm day and we go through our water quickly. Misreading the trail guide, I insist on a quarter mile detour in search of a spring. Venado protests, and can't help saying, "I told you, Papa," when I admit I've made a mistake. By the time we get to Cove Mountain it's late.

"Where did you kill the rattlesnake?"

"I don't know, must've been back there somewhere. I shouldn't have done it. It was an instinctive thing."

"Poppy?"

"Yeah?"

"Can we go to the Doyle?"

I hold up my hand to measure the sun. "It's late. Do you think we can make it?"

Venado nods.

"Okay, let's go. Walk fast." But as fast as we go, the sun goes down faster and we are still high up on the mountain when it dips below the horizon.

"We've got about half an hour of twilight. Go, go, go!"

Abruptly, the mountain drops off into the Susquehanna Valley, and we bounce down the steep switchbacked trail as fast as we dare, Venado in the lead.

"Don't run off the trail, Venado. It's a long drop." Ever since reaching Pennsylvania the trail has gotten rockier, and we have both taken our share of spills. "Let's be careful, my boy; this is not the time to fall."

We use up every last bit of light until we can no longer see the blazes, and all of a sudden we spill out onto flat ground—a parking lot full of tractor-trailers. We've lost the trail in the dark but manage to follow a dirt road out to a tarred road that leads to town. At a convenience store we buy a root beer and a gallon of spring water. We guzzle the root beer, passing it back and forth until it's gone; then, map and flashlight in hand, we hike as fast as we can into town, searching for the Doyle.

Up ahead, illuminated by streetlights and headlights, stands a venerable old building skirted by a wide porch, and from the railing hangs a sign: "Hikers Welcome."

The manager is just locking up when we get there.

"You just about missed me," he says, and leads us back into the old-fashioned taproom. We pay him thirty-two dollars and sign the register.

"We need fuel for our stove. Do you have HEET, or denatured alcohol?"

The manager hands me a gallon can of alcohol and a funnel. "Fill up outside in the alley."

Outside in the dark alley, Venado holds a flashlight as I pour fuel into our scratched and dirty sports drink bottle—marked with a skull and crossbones—spilling a few ounces on the ground. We return the gallon can and funnel to the manager and climb the stairs up to the third floor.

I run my fingers over the desiccated wood of the wainscoting and feel the dry wooden steps underfoot. "Geez, what a firetrap." But I'm relieved when we reach our room. "Right next to a fire escape, must be the best room in the house, and right across the hall from the bathroom. I like it."

The claw-footed tub is deep, the water hot, and after a hot bath, we share one of the well-worn beds. The mattress sinks almost to the floor.

"Ah, the Doyle," I say. "Setting the standard for hiker comfort." But Venado is already asleep, and I follow quickly.

After one of our most restful nights on the trail, we awaken to rain. At eight a.m. we walk down to the post office, pick up a resupply box, carry it back to the hotel, and dump the contents on the bed.

"Okay, okay," I say, as Venado looks on, "we need five dinners and lunches and six breakfasts." And we start to organize the food.

Venado picks out all the energy bars, gorp, and dried fruit for his pack, as I work on making three piles: One contains two huge bags of granola and powdered milk; another consists of eight bags of noodle soup, a package of rye crackers, eight ounces of cheese, a twelve-ounce pepperoni, a sixteen-ounce jar of peanut butter, and a pound of butter; the last pile consists of numerous plastic sandwich bags filled with mac and cheese, homemade dry soups, and dried hummus, flanked by a couple of cans of tuna. It's a more or less typical menu for the trail. We sort it out and go over it a couple of times, balancing our need for calories with our capacity for hauling all this up and down mountains.

I want to jettison the peanut butter, but Venado volunteers to carry it. We leave some couscous and a couple of soups in the hiker box—a box featured in many trail-friendly establishments where hikers can take what they need and leave what they don't. We pack our heavy bags and descend onto the dreary gray streets of a fading Pennsylvania town. Following white blazes painted on street signs, telephone poles, and guardrails, we cross two long bridges: one over the Juniata River, another over the Susquehanna. Often confused by reflectors and paint splotches that look like blazes, we navigate through a concrete maze of highway on-ramps and off-ramps until we reach the woods.

As the clouds begin spitting a light drizzle, we climb out of the gap on the eastern side, following a much gentler trail than the steep descent off Cove Mountain. Gradually, the overwhelming roar of the highways dulls into a background hum as we ascend the long switchbacks that give us ever loftier views of the great river below. The Susquehanna is to Pennsylvania what the Mississippi is to the United States; it cuts down through the center of the state, draining most of the land into the sea, as the Mississippi drains most of the country.

Clambering over wet rocks, we decide we need walking sticks, and we start watching the trail sides for likely candidates. Sticks abound out in the woods, but they need to be the right stuff: hard, light, and relatively straight. Venado chooses one, and I tell him to whack it on a tree to test its strength, which he does. He looks surprised when the end snaps off and whizzes past my head.

"Okay, we need to be more careful about that."

It takes time to find the right stick—it's something of an art—but Venado soon has an improvised hiking pole in hand to help him balance and pull himself up the mountain. I find one further on.

We seldom see other hikers on the trail, especially on cold rainy days, but up ahead we spot a guy in red shorts and white T-shirt descending down out of the gray, wet woods. We meet him amidst a tumble of dark rocks surrounded by black, naked trees. The guy's red floral shorts stand out.

I have on rain chaps and the heavy yellow slicker that John Rinehart gave me. Venado is equally protected from the weather, but this southbound hiker doesn't even have a hat on his balding head.

"I like those shorts," I say.

"Thanks. I got them in Hawaii."

"I believe it."

His name is Prairie Dog, and he explains he's on a mission to hike as far as the Maryland line. He's doing the entire trail in sections and he's almost done. He asks Venado where we're going.

"We're hiking the Appalachian Trail," Venado tells him.

"The whole thing?"

"Yep."

"How old are you?"

"Se . . . Eight."

"Where did you start?

I interrupt and give him a quick explanation of the plan.

Prairie Dog nods in approval. "I wish I could get my boy out here," he says, and starts to move past us.

"Check us out on Facebook," I say as he goes by, inviting him to look up our page. And on we go, hoping to cover eleven miles from Duncannon to Peters Mountain Shelter. Water, water everywhere and not a drop to drink. At the five-mile mark we pass up a chance to go down six hundred feet for water, deciding to press on for Peters Mountain instead. Three hours later, with daylight to spare, we arrive at what I call one of the trail's finest shelters. Its distinguishing features include a spacious second floor, a picnic table on a sheltered deck, and a stone stairway descending approximately 290 steps to a reliable spring.

There seems to be disagreement regarding the number of steps so we decide to count them. Busy talking, we forget to count on the way down, but we try on the way up, and when we get to the top we compare notes:

"Two hundred sixty," says Venado.

"Two hundred sixty? Where did you stop counting? I got two hundred eighty-five."

"I counted all that were together."

"Let's call it two seventy-five," I say. "I'm not going back down. We'll catch rainwater for the rest of what we need." Cook pot in hand, I stretch my arm out to catch a thread of water pouring off the roof.

Feeling deep relief to have made it to the dry and comfortable shelter, I take off my shoes and sit down at the picnic table, resting my aching feet. Venado inspects everything that's been left behind by other hikers: some socks, a tarp, magazines, a sleeping bag, and a big heavy poncho. He insists we sleep on the second floor, and I send him up there with our pads and sleeping bags.

After three nights in beds we return to sleeping on ensolite pads again. Venado drifts off quickly, while I turn over and over like a rotisserie chicken. We had chosen ensolite pads because they are, as I like to say, "half the weight, twice the warmth, and zero of the comfort of an inflatable pad." Besides, it still seems like winter and we need dependable warmth; an ensolite pad will never lose its air and leave us at risk of hypothermia.

Next morning we rise early and hit the trail. Clouds still hang above us but the rain has stopped. A couple of miles on, we shed our packs by a stream that winds through a rhododendron thicket, and sit down for breakfast.

"Eighteen miles today, Venado. Do you think we can do it?"

"Yeah."

Hiking up a wide stony path—an old road—we meet an older man coming down with a shovel in his hand. He stops, plants the point of the shovel between his feet, and leans on the handle.

"Where you fellas headin'?"

"Hoping to get to Rausch Gap."

"Oh, you've a bit of a hike then. There's good water up there," he says nodding back over his shoulder. "Go to the second spring, that's the best."

"We saw one back there that was all orange," says Venado.

"That's sulfur," says the old man, bending a bit to the boy. "It comes from the old coal mines." He explains to us how mule trains hauled coal from out of these mountains and down to the railroads, and how the villages here all died out after the railroads closed. "When you get close to Rausch Gap you'll see big piles of coal that they just left there."

We find the promised spring, a hand's breadth of clear water flowing from a pool surrounded by flat gray stones. I suggest we drink as much as we can before we fill up our bottles.

The trail angles steeply up. "God bless those mules hauling wagons up here. Brutal."

Near the top of the ridge we spot a sign marking the western end of the Horseshoe Trail.

"This is the Horseshoe Trail. Uncle Lou and Aunt Maribelle rode horses all the way out here from the farm in Collegeville."

"Who are Uncle Lou and Aunt . . . ?"

"My grandfather's brother and sister. That was sometime in the fifties, before even I was born."

"What did they do after they got here?"

"Rode back I guess."

"Are they still alive?"

"No, my boy, long dead."

Pennsylvania has a reputation as one of the hardest sections of the trail. Some people attribute that to the rocks, but having grown up there, I tend to think it's the monotony that wears people down. Walking along the rock-strewn waterless ridges with interstate highways droning on either side, the wreckage of the industrial revolution often visible, sometimes makes us have to work at feeling like we're in the wilderness. But we enjoy Pennsylvania; for me there's the nostalgia, for Venado the novelty, and for both of us the pure joy of being out here together—and in early spring without leaves on the trees we at least have views, which summer hikers find few and far between. Pennsylvania, home of Earl Shaffer, the first thru-hiker, defies the odds to become one of our favorite parts of the hike.

Farther on, we come to a sign that marks the vague remains of an abandoned village, Yellow Springs. On this dreary day, under heavy clouds and mist, the tumbled stone foundations and chimneys are barely discernable under dripping green shrubs.

"If it wasn't for this sign, I would probably never have noticed it."

"Poppy, why did they just go away?

"It says in the book they first started mining here in the eighteen hundreds, but the coal was not so good, and they shut down the railroad, and by nineteen twenty everyone was gone." We look around trying to spot more remains. "Seems like the houses would have stood up better. Our house is that old."

"It's all woods."

"That's what happens. Nature takes it all back."

We walk on together, and on the wide Pennsylvania trails we often walk side by side. Venado takes my hand and I smile. "I wonder how many father and son thru-hikers get to hike holding hands," I say, and we start swinging our arms in unison, which makes us laugh.

Later, off to our right, rise mountains of coal, covered with small trees.

"How much further, Poppy?"

"How much further do you think?"

"Two miles?"

"That'd be my guess. My feet hurt."

"Mine too."

"Really? How long have your feet hurt?"

"All day."

"Why didn't you tell me?"

"Because it doesn't matter."

At Rausch Gap we meet Bill. We call him "poor Bill" after he shows us his feet, all blistered and full of angry sores where the skin tore off. He's out for four days and has a four-inch-thick copy of *War and Peace* or some such tome, and a mountain of food, and heavy gear scattered all over the shelter.

"I walked twenty miles yesterday," he tells us. "My feet got soaking wet."

Venado looks at Bill's big pack and his trail-runner sneakers.

"Where you going?" I ask.

"Port Clinton," he says. "My girlfriend is picking me up there on Friday."

"That's where we're going too. But you need to be able to walk some eighteen-mile days to get there by Friday. Do you have any moleskin?"

"What's moleskin?"

I cut him some strips of moleskin. "Listen, Bill, I think you have a serious mismatch between pack weight and footwear. It's up to you, but I would recommend you hitch into the nearest town and mail at least twenty pounds of gear home, and maybe find a lighter book."

Next morning Bill is gone, but after hiking a mile we we spot him up ahead of us, hobbling along toward Swatara Creek. With our relatively light packs, we run down the trail after him like warriors attacking, as if we would club him to the ground and scalp him. But once we catch him we greet him warmly, and we all ford a flooded stream together. Venado crosses above the rushing water, balancing on a four-inch-diameter log, while Bill and I barefoot it across on submerged stepping stones. On the far side of Swatara Creek, we leave Bill sitting in the sun with his shoes off, and that's the last we see of him.

"Do you think he'll make it to Port Clinton, Poppy?"

"Not likely."

But we make it, racking up fifty-two miles in three days on the rocky ridges. And along the way we pass a stone boundary marker for Berks County. "This is where it all started for me," I tell Venado. "These are the woods I ran when I was a boy. My grandparents bought a place up here after the state took our farm."

"Is this where you saw the Native American?"

"The ghost?"

"Yeah, you told me about him; when you were a kid, you saw him."

I nod. "Yeah, that was way south of here, near a spring." And I tell the story again, of the chill in my spine, sensing a presence, and there out of the corner of my eye a figure, and when I'd turned, it was gone. But I never forgot it—something there had reached deep into me.

Later we come across a marker from Fort Dietrich Snyder, an outpost during the French and Indian War. "This is from the war in *The Last of the Mohicans*. It was all the way down here too. The king of England had set the land west of the Alleghenies aside for the native tribes, but that didn't stop the French traders and colonial expansionists from fighting for it." It's a subject dear to my heart and I explain to Venado how our ancestors most likely fought in New York, the old French colony of Acadia—now Maine—and the Canadian Maritimes. "Some folks say how they had family on both sides of the Civil War; we had family on both sides of the French and Indian War, and the Revolution, too."

Down in Port Clinton we pick up a resupply box with a serious water filter that weighs over a pound. We mail some excess food ahead to Delaware Water Gap, buy fuel, grab burgers at Wendy's, and then climb over a low ridge to Windsor Furnace. "Seems like there were a lot of furnaces in Pennsylvania once upon a time," Venado says.

"Yeah, I wonder why? There must be lots of iron in the ground. I think I remember somebody, maybe my Uncle Pete, telling me that compasses can't always be trusted up here because of all the iron in the ground."

"Did they use coal?"

"I think they used charcoal, like it said at Pine Grove."

Later, I check the Internet and tell Venado that it was Pennsylvania's abundant hardwood forests and ore, together, that made the furnaces here viable. "But by the early eighteen hundreds, the charcoal making was unsustainable. The colliers, as they were called, were harvesting an acre of forest a day per furnace, with hundreds of furnaces in operation. So they switched to coke, and now the woods have grown back."

"Coke?" Venado asks and it's obvious he's thinking Coca-Cola.

"No, coke, it's like charcoal I think, made from soft coal."

Next morning we hike nine miles to a road and hitch to the Creekside Cultural Center, to take our first whole day off the trail—a zero day.

Of all the places I have researched prior to the hike, the Creekside Cultural Center comes closest to MacKaye's vision of the communally owned camps where people can learn rural skills, walk in the woods, and invest in a community.

I had sent the director, Tori Odhner, a copy of MacKaye's essay "An Appalachian Trail."

"Wow, this is SOO cool!" she'd written back, excited. "And SO much what we are trying to do ourselves. Thank you for sharing it with me. I think I will include this with my next newsletter to our membership."

When we arrive, Tori gives us the tour. The place is small, consisting of a house she rents out to prospective members of her intended intentional community and a barn used for various events, including self-help groups, boy scout meetings, and weekly concerts.

We find her dream, like MacKaye's, still far from reality. The hot baths and comforts we'd imagined evaporate when she offers us couches in the unheated barn. And baths? She has to talk to the renters of the house, who agree to let us take a bath. We use all the available hot water to fill the tub and soak in it together. But it turns out to be a great time once we let go of the comfort thing. Tori's brother, Wade, teaches Venado how to make rope from basswood bark. The renters' kids come over to play.

"Tonight we're having a singer-songwriter from Virginia, Andrew McKnight," Tori tells me. "And tomorrow we're having a bluegrass duo from North Carolina, and a potluck!"

On Saturday evening Andrew McKnight takes the stage and sings his heart out for us. The renters' kids can't sit still, so Tori kicks them out, but Venado sits rapt in his chair. Sunday morning, my brother Jim comes up from Newtown Square, near Philadelphia, and Venado and I return to the trail for a short hike with him. Jim wants to go farther, but the damp, raw weather takes the fun out of it, and Venado and I need a rest. We hijack him off the trail and get him to take us to lunch at Cabela's in Hamburg. We order things like buffalo burgers, and later, while we explore the store, my brother expresses surprise at our fascination with the flintlocks in the gun department.

"I didn't know you were into this," he says.

"Oh yeah, if we ever have an extra $1,000 we're going to get one of these," I say, sighting down the barrel of a blue mountain rifle.

I buy Venado a green cap with gold lettering that says: "Cabela's: the World's Foremost Outfitter." "What does that mean?" he asks, and I explain.

Jim drops us back at the barn, and heads home. The Sunday afternoon potluck has brought out a small crowd, but they bring plenty of food, and Venado and I consume almost an entire cherry pie before settling down to listen to more music. The duo Mandolin Orange—Emily Frantz and Andrew Marlin—has come all the way from North Carolina to play to a dozen listeners in a cold barn.

They play with their down jackets on, totally unplugged, not even a microphone, but the old wood and stone surrounding them holds their songs warmly. They sound sweet harmonizing in that cathedral-like structure.

"This is so pure Pennsylvania," I say to Venado. "It reminds me of the folk festivals we used to go to in high school."

He nods, and sits there tapping his foot.

That night we get the big bed in the heated basement. It turns out Tori doesn't actually live at Creekside; she's gone back to her house in Philadelphia.

Monday morning we head off into the rain again with packs full of leftovers. Taking a rest has restored us, and we pass our intended destination, pushing on to a restaurant/campground we've read about in the guide. But it's closed, and for the first time, we set up our tent in the rain. It's still raining when we wake up, and I stuff the sopping wet tent into my pack. The wind picks up, and the rocks get pretty bad.

When navigating wet watermelon-sized rocks that cover the trail, every step requires a thought; walking becomes a series of precision placements of each foot, and we pick our way along like that for an hour before the rain lets up and gives us a chance to stop for breakfast. Distracted, I put my brand-new knife down on a big log, and a mile or two later I think of it there. We stop and debate whether to go back or not, opting to forsake the knife.

Walking ahead of me, Venado leads the way across an exposed ridge of wet windswept boulders. I watch him clamber slowly and steadily onward, crossing what many might consider treacherous terrain, and balancing against the intermittent gusts. We make it seven miles to Bake Oven Knob Shelter and take a long lunch.

"What do you think, Venado, six more miles to Outerbridge?"

"Ummm. Sure."

"No rain, no pain, no Maine." And once again we boot up and strike out into the rain, paralleling a massive wall of boulders, until the trail turns and up we go, into the wind, with the rain now mixed with snow.

"Poppy, I left my stick."

I turn to look back, take a step, slip, and go down hard, landing with my head right next to a sharp pointed rock. I get up slowly, staring at the rock.

"Well we're not going back; we'll have to find you another." But it's getting cold, and coming off the wall we miss the blazes and have to climb back up to relocate the trail.

"Two miles to go, Venado." In spite of the harsh weather, Venado bounces along humming—every day in the woods brings something memorable.

"Look," Venado says. "A turtle."

I look around. "Where?"

"Here in these rocks, see?"

I look down at the formation and see the shape of a turtle in a jumble of rocks on the ground. "Wow, that really is a turtle."

Further on Venado asks: "Poppy?"

"Yeah?"

"Before we were human did we walk on our toes?"

"What?"

"Did we walk on our toes, like animals?"

"I don't know. I wasn't around then."

"But like in fossils. Can they tell?"

"Maybe. I don't know."

My mind is on other things. "Listen, when we get to the shelter I want you to change into your dry clothes and get right into your sleeping bag."

We arrive at a sign pointing off the trail to our right and hurry along a sloping path of wet gravel to the welcome dry shelter—George Outerbridge—we add its name to the litany and like Devils Racecourse it becomes one we can never forget; the names of places that give us shelter from the rain and snow never escape us. Venado, shivering, changes clothes and crawls into his bag while I start cooking. We plan to pick up a resupply in Danielsville the following day, so we feast. While Venado hunkers in his sleeping bag, I get creative, mixing up a dry meat, couscous, hummus, and butter stew, and making grilled cheese on cracker sandwiches drenched in butter, followed by mulled apple cider mixes we got from the folks at Creekside.

The following morning breaks sunny and cool for us, and we roll light-footed down into the Lehigh Valley. Back at a shelter we shared with a southbound hiker named Bunyan—an outrageous snorer who kept me awake all night—Bunyan had told us about the difficulty of climbing out of Lehigh Gap. But on a warm day with almost empty packs, we have a blast rock-climbing up out of the steep gorge. On the ridge above the river a big turkey has his tail all fanned out, gobbling. But when we shout in unison "a turkey!" the tom bails into the woods—that's how it usually goes with wildlife.

Below us in the valley, the remains of a zinc smelter that polluted these mountains to death sits with its blackened stacks and corrugated roofs rusting; behind it flows the Lehigh River, and along the river runs a double ribbon of train tracks with some gondolas idle and empty on a siding. "It looks like the day the world stood still," I say, staring down at the bleak scene.

On top of the mountain we meet a trail angel, Carl Rush, who drives us to the Danielsville post office for our resupply box and then back out to the trail. Towards dark, after hiking several miles without water, and too far from a shelter, Venado reaches a dirt road ahead of me and flags down a ride.

"I couldn't believe I saw this little kid hitchhiking," says the driver. He takes us to the home of yet another trail angel, John Stempa, who gives us water, cake, and a place to set up our tent. We get to sign the same register as Earl Shaffer, and after we're settled, John asks us if we want to lie down in the driveway while his nine-year-old son, a cycle-cross racer, jumps his bike off a ramp and sails over us. "All the hikers do it. Go ahead."

Venado shakes his head. He's not into it. Neither am I. "No thanks, John. We take enough risks already."

Two days later, we reach the end of Pennsylvania—Delaware Water Gap—and make our way to a famous free hostel in a church basement. We have it all to ourselves, and Venado, picking through the shelves, finds a book about geology: volcanoes and all different types of rock. Venado can't get enough of the geology book and insists that I read it with him. But we have things to do. I convince him to put the book down and we walk over to the post office to pick up a food box and then cross the street to visit Edge of the Woods Outfitters. I tap into the store's open Wi-Fi signal and start checking my email. Venado wanders around touching everything. I call my wife to see what we need for gear. I want to get a bigger cook pot for when Venado's older sister joins us. Between Internet surfing and phone calls we're there for almost an hour, but before I can get all our issues resolved, the owner comes over and asks if I plan on buying anything.

"I don't know yet."

"Well, if you're not going to buy anything, can you please leave?"

I look at him. "What?"

"Can you leave, please?"

"You're throwing us out?"

The guy shrugs. "We have other things to do."

I keep looking at him. "What?"

"Otherwise we have to watch you."

"You have to watch us?"

Venado stands there watching and listening.

"Come on," I say and take him by the hand. "We have to go."

We take our food box back to the free hostel and I write a frustrated ode on my iPhone.

Delaware Water Gap, April 2, 2010

Ode to the Woods Edge Outdoors Store

You don't know us. We come out of the woods stinking and quite scruffy, and roll into your camping store like we're right at home. Tap into your Wi-Fi signal, start banging out emails while pawing all your goods with the dirt still under our fingernails. And so surprised when you say, look, buy something or be on your way. Ah well. We didn't know what we needed, we were waiting to hear from our support team. It was a shame. Like getting kicked out of the candy store for smudging the glass on the cases.

Onward without that new cookpot we wanted.

Afterwards, I organize our supplies, and take a pound of butter up to the church office to see if they have a use for it. The pastor, a middle-aged woman, is irritated with me. "You say you're thru-hiking? In jeans?"

I look down at my jeans.

Later, she comes to visit us in the basement and I tell her about the outdoors store.

"Don't judge them too hard," she says. "There was a man murdered here two days ago, burned to death in his business. It's got everyone on edge."

Venado keeps his face in the geology book. After she leaves, he and I read it some more, along with another book about the formation of the gap. Towards dusk we wander up to a little restaurant and buy our last Pennsylvania meal: birch beer, hot dogs, and shoofly pie.

"Let's get back to the hostel," I suggest once we finish our food. "I want to leave here as early as possible tomorrow."

At dawn we are on the I-80 bridge, hemmed in between a concrete rail and a stream of cars and semis tearing up the morning. I try to take photos, but the cliffs rising fifteen hundred feet on the New Jersey side lie in shadow, silhouetted by the rising sun. We can see the ribbons of different colored stone that tell the region's geological story, but my iPhone camera cannot

"My brother and I first came up here in the seventies," I tel "I would organize camping trips and bring all our friends fro school up here to climb on the cliffs. We didn't understand any about that stuff in the geology book, the smashing of tectonic plate the Paleozoic era, or the mixing of the gravel quartzite conglomerat not even the scouring of the Wisconsin Glacier during the last ice age."

"You didn't know about the ice age?"

"We didn't know the glaciers reached this far. But I can remember what those rocks smelled and felt like on a hot spring day. We used to set up ropes and go rappelling down. I can still hear the *zzzzz* of the rope and the smack of our boots on the rock."

"Can we climb them?"

"Not today."

As often happens on the trail, we keep walking, making an unre-markable departure from a remarkable place, but we have a date to pick up Venado's sister at Bear Mountain in a week, and we have to make the miles.

5

...NHATTAN
SKYLINE

We've left Pennsylvania behind and Venado has just revealed a remarkable fact about New Jersey, our fourth state so far.

"One bear per square meter?" I ask.

"That's what that lady said: New Jersey has one bear per square meter."

"That sounds kinda crowded."

"Yeah, that would be a lot of bears—excuse me, coming through."

I'm laughing. "I think maybe she meant one per square *mile*."

"Probably."

We're climbing out of the gap on the New Jersey side, the Mount Tammany side—Mount Minsi forms the Pennsylvania-side rampart. The trail follows a ravine along a stream shrouded by tall hemlocks. It's become a habit for us to flip up the tips of the lowest boughs, and sure enough we find them flecked with the little white snowflakes of the hemlock woolly adelgid.

Farther on, we come upon a vaguely familiar spot that opens a door to my youth. "Look, look, see that flat spot up there? I camped right there when I was in high school. We climbed down through here and up the other side there to get warm in the morning sun." I stop to look around at the place I remember from over thirty years earlier. "This is so strange."

But for Venado, the only story Delaware Water Gap holds is what is happening in the present moment. "Poppy, I don't have the same feeling as you do about this place, and Pennsylvania."

We emerge from the woods onto the shore of Sunfish Pond and read on a plaque that it is a glacial lake, one of the southernmost left behind by the retreating ice sheets of the Wisconsin Glaciations. It seems like a good place for lunch, and so we sit down on a tree that stretches its trunk out over the pond. Venado drops his cheese into the water and I make him fish it out and eat it.

"We didn't carry that this far to drop it into Sunfish Pond," I tell him. "Besides, we've only got just enough to get to Unionville." But late in afternoon we stumble onto the Mohican Outdoor Center—and decide to buy into the all-you-can-eat lasagna buffet they're offering, including two pieces each of pumpkin pie for dessert

Part of the Appalachian Mountain Club, MOC is a version of the camps MacKaye envisioned, but more for people who enjoy the woods as a relaxing place to spend a weekend rather than weeks or months. MOC offers free camping for thru-hikers, and we camp there. The meal has helped augment our meager food supply and Venado and I enjoy the conversation

Helping to clean up afterwards, I grab the last slice of pie, plop some whipped cream on it, and take it outside. I find Venado and offer him the pie. "You ready for this?"

Venado smiles. "Yeah!"

We talk about food and think about food all the time now, and we've gotten so skinny I have to poke new holes in our belts. "Give me your knife there, Venado."

He passes it to me.

"Man, I haven't been this skinny since high school," I say. After cinching my belt, I fold the knife and slip it into my pocket.

"Hey, that's my knife," Venado says, demanding it back.

"Get outta here—your mom loaned it to you."

"So it's mine."

"Okay, it's yours. I'm going to carry it for now."

"But you lost yours."

We argue over who will have the knife, but it's in my pocket so I prevail for the time being.

The trail runs fairly level along Kittatinny Ridge, with the Delaware River off to our left. A small herd of deer comes charging up the side of the ridge on our right and veers away in a panic.

I'm laughing with delight. "Wow, I never imagined New Jersey would be so sweet—beautiful views, wildlife."

"And pumpkin pie."

That evening I inform Venado that I forgot our toothbrushes at MOC, and so I show him how to make what I know as an "Indian toothbrush" from a twig of gray birch. I cut a twig about six inches long, thinner than a pencil, sharpen one end for a toothpick, and peel the bark away on the last three quarters of an inch on the other end. I hand in to Venado. "Here, chew on this end until you break up the fibers and make it a brush."

He takes it and gnaws on the end. "Mmmm. This tastes good, like wintergreen."

I make another for myself and show Venado the technique.

The next morning we eat breakfast at a deli near a road crossing. "We better start eating our own food soon or we'll be carrying it all the way to New York," I say, as we head back toward the woods, passing a sign on a lawn that says: "Please don't 'Hike' on the grass."

"Poppy?"

"Yeah?"

"We forgot to buy toothbrushes."

"Hmmm. I guess we'll have to use twigs again."

We push on late into the day, arriving at High Point State Park at dusk. The park office doors are locked, so we get water from an outdoor spigot and continue across the road into the woods.

Venado wants to stop. "We need to camp here," he says.

"It's illegal," I tell him. "We'll have to be very stealthy."

"Okay," he says as he dumps his pack, clearly unwilling to go any further.

We set up our tent and eat a cold supper of trail mix and Clif Bars. I put all our food into my pack and climb up into a tree. I ask Venado to pass the heavy pack up and it's all he can do to lift it to my outstretched

Burial of sticks killed in a tornado

hand. Together we get it into the tree, more or less secure from bear depredations. A car pulls into the park office parking lot across the road and its headlights shine in to where we are hiding.

"Let's be still," I say, and we wait. Eventually the car goes away. We fall asleep. No bears come by during the night.

The days get hotter; a freak heat wave drives temperatures up into the nineties. Nearing Unionville, New York, we pass through a strange area where tall ash and oak trees lie flattened, as if mowed down.

"Tornado touched down there last year," a local tells us when we get into the town.

In Unionville, we pick up a resupply box at the post office and the postmistress, Tina, asks us if we would like a drink of cold water.

"We sure would," I say, and she disappears around back, returning with ice-cold water in plastic cups, which she refills after we drink them down. We sort out our resupply box at a pizza restaurant, wash socks in the bathroom, and charge my iPhone. "Is this okay?" I ask. "We're sort of moving in."

"No problem," the pizza guys say. Afterwards we buy fuel at the mayor's house in what is billed as one of the friendliest towns on the trail.

Road-walking out of town, Venado stops. "My tooth is really loose." And suddenly he's holding a bloody white nugget in his hand.

"Congratulations, Venado! You lost your first tooth on the Appalachian Trail." I take a photo of his new smile, and when I pick up a Wi-Fi signal, I send the picture to his mom.

The next day, hiking with heavy packs in the heat, we follow the trail rising alongside a rushing stream. Sweaty and hot, we breathe heavily, watching the clear water cascading through a narrow ravine, spilling over rock ledges into inviting pools.

"We could swim in that, Venado."

"Yeah."

We dump our packs and climb down to a shallow pool and dare each other to go completely under in the frigid water. We go under and pop up breathless. Shivering and refreshed, we are just getting our clothes back on when a couple of young women in skirts and makeup climb awkwardly up the trail, followed by their boyfriends. They look confused, eyeing the two of us.

We have taken on the air and patina of thru-hikers, even when freshly washed. My beard, Venado's long hair, all dripping, and our dirty packs resting against a tree, all speak of miles, and the trail as a lifestyle.

"Hi."

"Hi, what are you guys doing?" one of the girls asks.

"Swimming."

"Here?"

"Yeah, you should try it," I suggest as Venado grins up at them.

The girls give us lipstick-coated smiles. "Okay," says one. But it doesn't mean she's going in.

Again we hike till it's almost dark and take our chances with the bears. Low-flying jets from the Newark airport roar down on us through the night, and when I get up to pee, I don't even need a flashlight because of all the reflected glow from the nearby cities.

The next night, we find ourselves camped on a dry rock ridge with only a sip of water left between us. I hang my pack, stuffed with food, in a gnarled pine—scant protection from a serious bear, but it's the best we can do. It's a rough night: poorly fed, thirsty, and sleeping on a rock. Then comes the splatter of rain on the tent, followed by a flash of lightning and thunder rumbling in the distance. I lie there counting the seconds between the lightning and the thunder, listening to the rain batter the tent, wondering if we will have to break camp in the dark and rain and beat it to safer ground.

But the lightning diminishes, the thunder fades into the distance, and before dawn the stars twinkle above us. We hit the trail as soon as we can see it and scramble down into a valley where we filter water from a stream within sight of a building complex.

"They say this filter can make even your pee drinkable," I tell Venado.

"Can I pump it?"

"No, my boy, it's too hard. It wears *me* out."

Coming up the next ridge, entering Harriman State Park, Venado stops.

"What is it?"

"Poppy, it's a vulture!"

"Where?" I tip my hat back as I step up behind Venado, looking far ahead.

"There." Venado points right in front of us and there it is, a black-headed vulture, standing over two feet tall, hopping with half-spread wings from rock to rock.

"It must be guarding its nest."

We stand there, watching a bird that up till now we have only seen floating on wings held in a stiff V, either drifting below us across valleys or hanging like an ornament in the sky. But here it has personality.

"Hello," I say.

"Hi," Venado joins in.

The vulture does not respond.

"Go on, Venado, she'll get out of your way."

As Venado steps tentatively toward the large bird with its sharp curved beak, the vulture flaps and hops awkwardly away and past white blazes painted on the rocks; it had obviously overlooked them when it built its nest.

Further on, we cross Cats Rock, and a raven flies out from a crevice. Venado, walking ahead, spots its nest.

"Poppy, there. It came from right over there. There's a nest!"

We hurry across the smooth granite boulders.

"Over this way, I think."

"No, it's here." Venado runs to the edge and looks down. "It's a nest!" He calls back to me.

Only three feet beneath him, almost within reach, five blind raven chicks squawk for their mother.

I take a quick look, and a picture. "Come on, we should leave them alone."

We race along as fast as we can, trying to get to Bear Mountain before dark, but the trail through Harriman holds many surprises. It leads straight up and over every steep hill in the park. Coming off one, we find our first trail magic: an energy bar left on a stump—blueberry crisp flavor, which we have never tried. "Do you want to cut or choose?" I ask Venado.

"Choose," he says.

Just as well, because I have the knife. I carefully cut the bar in half, trying to make each piece equal. Venado looks them over.

"Sometimes when you cut I take the smaller piece," I remind him, but he takes the slightly bigger one. We have been on the trail close to a month, and have spent more time together, just the two of us, than we had ever spent before. After years of me having been gone working or traveling, now we do everything together: eat, sleep, walk, and split energy bars.

At one point we come to a fork in the trail; the white blazes go up a cliff, blue blazes mark the "easy trail."

I smile. "Oh cool, we get a break."

"Oh no," Venado says. "We're thru-hikers, we don't go the easy way."

I give him a surprised look. "Go on up then, I'll pass you your pack." He slips off his little pack, hands it to me, and climbs up the steep face. When I pass him his pack he turns away. "Hold on there, you have to take mine." I lift my pack up to him. "Can you handle it?"

"Yeah," he says through gritted teeth.

Later in the day we step out into the open on top of Black Mountain, and I stare off to the southeast. "There, Venado, look. That must be New York City." And in the hazy distance a tiny patch of towers breaks the smooth horizon.

"It looks like spires in the desert," he says.

I take a video, but we can't see the city in it; it's too far away. "Here Venado, put out your finger and hold it right here . . . " and I guide his finger to where the city is in the frame. "You can't see it, but there it is," I narrate, and then shut the camera off.

"How about that, huh? New York City from the AT."

"Yeah, teeny tiny New York City."

The parks we pass through on our approach to the city—Worthington and Stokes State Forests in New Jersey, Harriman State Park in New York—have all been built around land donated from wealthy patrons. Millionaire industrialist Charles C. Worthington bought most of what is now Worthington State Forest to use as a private hunting preserve. Sunfish Pond supplied the water for his nearby mansion, Buckwood Lodge. He restocked the woods with thousands of deer and pheasants and renamed Sunfish Pond "Buckwood Lake" while he owned it.

In 1909, New Jersey governor Edward Stokes donated five hundred acres to the state of New Jersey. The state added more land to what is now Stokes State Forest.

But the gem of all these parks is Harriman State Park, forty-three thousand acres of prime real estate within sight of New York City, a gift from Mary Williamson Averell Harriman. Her son, nineteen-year-old W. Averell Harriman, who would later play a role in Franklin D. Roosevelt's administration, handed over the deed and a check for a million dollars to the New York governor in 1910.

Financially and politically, these folks were giants; they lived in a world apart from the masses and wielded power in ways most people could barely conceive of. But the trees, the ravens, and the wildlife do not know why they have been spared or who has spared them. And Venado and I, when we look down at the tiny city, can see the design of the metropolitan utopia in the midst of a vast forest—nature—that will someday reclaim it.

"Just imagine, someday New York will be just like Yellow Springs."

"Huh?"

"Not in our lifetimes, Venado. But all civilizations crumble eventually, and the forests grow over them."

We hurry on. Coming down to the road at the foot of Bear Mountain at the bitter end of twilight, we can barely see the blazes. We blow on our whistles in case Venado's mom is there. But when we reach the road we find it dark and deserted.

"Look," says Venado, pulling a piece of paper out from under a rock. There is just light enough to make it out:

Wait here, I'll be back.

A few minutes later a lone car comes down the road and pulls over in front of us, headlights on. Venado's mom jumps out and gives her boy a big, tearful hug.

6

THE WAR CLUB

"The creatures of the forest constitute a warring society . . . In unraveling the forest civilization we reveal the contrasts of our own."
—Benton MacKaye

After two months on the trail, we take a two-night break with family in Westchester County. My wife has brought me a new knife, a very simple one with a single blade, not as nice as the one I lost, but I'm content. I've made a commitment to stop complaining, and she's watching me. She and I work on setting up our daughter for three weeks on the trail. It's part of the deal, and we joke that Venado's sister is "court ordered."

"Mom has to go to work in Canada," I tell her. "You have to come hiking with us."

On May 11, she sets off with us, bearing the self-chosen trail name Bluebell. She has blue pants, blue rain gear, a blue hat, blue gloves, and a blue Deuter youth pack, the Fox 30. "I like your pack," I tell her. "I'd like one like that." But I have to stick with my larger pack to compensate for Venado's tiny one. Fortunately Bluebell can carry twenty percent of her weight and then some, and I am relieved to have her with us. She takes over hauling the granola, powdered milk, and cook pot, and with her on the team we can afford the weight of a cell phone and charger. With her hair done up in pigtails and her new blue gear, Bluebell starts off in high spirits.

We get dropped off right where Venado and I had been picked up two nights earlier, and after hugs and goodbyes to their mom, the kids and I cross the road to the trail that leads up Bear Mountain. Walking ahead, Venado and Bluebell come upon a pileated woodpecker, a black and white crow-sized bird with a startling red crest. It's busy tearing apart a rotten tree and they surprise it and get a close look before it flies away screaming.

On the other side of the mountain, the trail runs through the Bear Mountain Zoo, where forlorn animals, including a cage-worn pileated woodpecker, stare listlessly from behind bars and fences.

"Their pileated woodpecker doesn't look as good as the one we saw on the mountain," Venado observes, and Bluebell and I agree.

As thru-hikers, we do not have to pay the toll when we cross the Hudson River on the venerable Bear Mountain Bridge. "See how this works?" I ask, pointing up at all the cables. "It's a suspension bridge, like that footbridge we crossed in New Jersey, Venado. This was the longest suspension bridge of the day, when it was built."

"When was that?"

"I don't know, eighteen something." The kids stop in the middle to look up and down the river. On the far side we make our way back into the woods. Setting an easy pace for our first day together, we head for a monastery only a few miles away, but we arrive weeks too early for camping. The monastery has yet to turn on the outside water for hikers, and so we improvise, drawing water from a rest room in the main building and camping on gravel under a picnic pavilion.

Gentle as we try to be on Bluebell, we find her crying in her sleeping bag as darkness falls. "I want to go home."

"Not an option," I tell her. "You're with us."

And so we walk across Putnam County, coaxing Bluebell into the fold. By the third day she has found her stride and we shoot for eighteen miles. "Nineteen if you count the hike out of Fahnestock State Park," Venado reminds us. We had gone a mile out of our way to Fahnestock because Bluebell wanted to stay there—but it was closed. Heading for Morgan Stewart Shelter, we meet a middle-aged woman hiking alone.

"War Clubs of the Americas"

Her lightweight, fairly high-end gear indicates she's done her homework and might be out for the long haul.

Her name is Marie, she says when we ask, but we're not interested in her civilizee name; we want her trail name. "Old Fool," she says, and we hike together to a shelter and have lunch. "I bought this alcohol stove," she says, showing us a forty-dollar ultralight stove. "But it doesn't work."

"Can I try?" I ask. She assents, and I fill the stove with fuel, letting some alcohol spill around the outside of it. I set the whole works ablaze—the stove flares up but quickly settles to a steady burn. "There, it works. You have to heat the stove a little first."

She's delighted, and thrilled to meet two children planning to spend months on the trail. She asks us many questions about education, and how far we hike every day. Walking along together, we learn that she is out hiking for charity, and shooting for seventy miles.

"Do you mind if I hike along with you?" she asks.

We welcome her company but warn her that we move right along. "Can you keep up?"

"I'll try," she says. And she does, valiantly. But after a few miles it's game over, and we never see her again. We leave her a note in the next shelter log and rename her "Chutzpah," because she is not old, or a fool.

Most of the time things go smoothly; Bluebell gets up early, stays organized, and hikes better than Venado and me. But her attitude leaves a bit to be desired. "I want to go home," she says—often.

"Well keep walking; we're headed that way," I tell her.

Normally, Bluebell and Venado have fun playing together. We teach Bluebell how to make a toothbrush from the wintergreen-flavored gray birch. The kids cut a grapevine loose at its base and make a swing over a shallow brook, and they laugh when Venado slips and falls in. One cold morning we find a golden salamander frozen on the ground, and we pass it around, breathing our warm breath onto it in cupped hands till it starts to squiggle; Venado puts it down and it scurries away under the moss. Venado makes a point of letting Bluebell know how wonderful life in the woods is, and how happy he is, though he might have been better off keeping that to himself.

In the mornings she shoulders her pack impatiently. "Come on, Venado, my god you are *so* slow. Dad, tell him to hurry up." When she cooks she refuses to let him help. "No, you'll spill it." Venado, admittedly, is slow to get up in the morning, and not always attentive when cooking.

At Ten-Mile Shelter, a beautiful campsite in Connecticut, we decide to quit hiking and enjoy some play time, but Venado takes so long to write a journal entry, his homeschooling assignment, that the day winds down without much play after all, and Bluebell harangues him about the wasted time.

I send an email to my wife: "She treats him the way you treat me; it's hard to watch."

She writes back, something to the effect that I have not been a picnic either, and I have to admit, it's true.

Passing trough Connecticut, I pick up a text from an old friend who goes by the trail name KlifyBoy. We haven't seen each other in seventeen years but he wants to come out and hike with us.

"Why not?" I say. The kids need a diversion, and I need another adult to talk to. "Sure, come on out," I text back, and we meet on the trail the next day.

Since we'd last spoken, KlifyBoy had gotten divorced. "I just realized I wasn't happy, and I didn't want to keep living that way," he says as we lag back behind Venado and Bluebell. I hint at some similar sentiments, but my friend offers me sage advice. "You've got two beautiful kids," he says. "Think long and hard before you make any big decisions."

Venado and Bluebell keep me focused on the present moment. We become students of rock and its various formations. We are learning at what angle our boots can grip the various types of rock, wet or dry. We read geological history in swirls of old lava flows, glacial scars, ice cracks, and the steady action of sand and water that carves perfect circular holes in the granite along the Housatonic River. And we know so little about what we see until someone tells us what we're looking at. "Those are garnets," KlifyBoy tells us as we puzzle over a boulder studded with dark crystals.

KlifyBoy leaves us early the first day with an offer to buy us steaks if we can make it to Belter's Campsite before dark. The race is on; we make good time until we come to Guinea Brook and find it flooded. While preparing to ford the high-running stream, Venado, who is not keen on the idea, spots a big fallen hemlock further upstream. Spanning the thirty-foot gap between two steep banks, the tree offers us a bridge a good twelve feet above the rock-strewn creek. We make our way up to it, and Venado crosses first, straddling the wide trunk and inching along with his pack on. Bluebell starts across with her pack on.

"I can't do it."

"Can you do it without your pack?" I ask.

"Yeah, I think so."

After she makes it to the other side, I start across with my pack on, pushing hers ahead of me. Once out on the log I realize the bark is loose. "Geez, you guys" I say, "if I had know how loose this bark was I wouldn't have let you go."

But it's worth the risk, because that steak dinner proves to be our finest meal on the trail. "I recommend the double-cut filet mignon," KlifyBoy tells me. I look at the price. "Really, go for it," he says, and I do. That steak, combined with my friend's sage counsel, restores me in body and soul.

Two days later we cross the border into Massachusetts, the prettiest state, according to Bluebell, and I take a slew of pictures and videos of the kids. Up on a ridge overlooking the Connecticut-Massachusetts border, I have my iPhone camera pointed at Bluebell.

"Why are we up here?" I ask.

"To see what giants see!" she responds enthusiastically.

"And breathe *oxygen*!" adds Venado, not to be outdone.

"And where are you two going?"

"To the shelter!" shouts Bluebell. "Only half a mile, let's go!"

"One point one miles," Venado corrects her.

"Whatever. Come on, let's go."

And it strikes me as I watch them run off ahead of me how much I truly love my children, and that the very best I can do for them at this stage of their young lives is hang on to the good we've got.

It has taken five hundred miles to get that meager stroke of inspiration into my head. But though it may seem simple in theory, it is difficult in practice—so I practice.

Halfway through Massachusetts, we stop at Moon in the Pond Farm, listed in *The Thru-Hikers' Companion* as a place where the owner, Dom Palumbo, will trade homegrown organic food for work. The thought of a table piled high with delicious farm food inspires us to call Dom, and he sends a young farmer to pick us up. When we arrive at Moon in the Pond, an old New England farm with a Cape house and a small barn, everyone is just sitting down to a simple lunch of egg salad, garden salad, and bread. We meet Dom, a small, energetic man in his fifties. He used to run his farm as "certified organic," he tells us, but now he certifies himself. "If Dole and Del Monte can get certified organic," he says, sitting in his rustic kitchen, "then certification becomes meaningless. It's not something I want to be a part of anymore."

Dom tries to avoid using machines on the farm—which we appreciate—so we spend the afternoon shoveling manure out a sheep stall and moving a ton of hay, one bale at a time. For supper Dom feeds us each a hot dog, some beans, noodles, and salad. I look around for bread, mustard, and things like that, but as Dom says, he likes to pay calorie for calorie, and so he sets a spare table. Later I carp about scant rations, but the kids don't care. They love feeding the goats and walking with the cows on Moon in the Pond Farm—and I have to admit, the place has a very calming feel to it. And when Dom takes us back to the trail the next day he gives us some apples and a bag of tortilla chips.

We make good time crossing Massachusetts, but, as always, we take time to talk to strangers and investigate our surroundings. We meet a paramedic who says he comes out to the trail every chance he can to clear his head. I ask if he has heard of MacKaye. "I don't read much," says the medic.

"MacKaye thought the trail would be a good place for folks to heal emotionally."

"Huh."

Coming out of North Adams, we meet a man named Bob Guerney, hiking with his son. "You're lucky to meet me," he says. "No one knows this part of the trail as well as I do. I've been walking it for sixty-six years [since he was five years old] and I can say it's the only thing around here that hasn't changed."

At Upper Goose Pond Cabin we find several saplings labeled "American Chestnut: *Castenea dentata*." Venado wants to know if I remember the chestnuts. "When I was little, in the sixties, I remember groves of dead trees and hearing my parents or somebody say something about chestnuts. I think they were groves of dead chestnuts. Remember at Bear Mountain? It said all the guardrails for the road up there were made of chestnut."

"Yeah," the kids nod.

Camped on the porch of Upper Goose, an AMC hut, we filter water from the pond and make mac and cheese with tuna. Just before dark another hiker comes striding in, hiking poles clicking, long legs sticking out from shorts, gaiters to the knee. He comes up onto the porch with a greeting as slender as his body and gaunt bearded face. We've already eaten, and so we watch attentively as he quickly goes about the business of cooking his supper. He uses a pocket rocket butane stove but has the same MSR titanium cook pot that we use, and he cooks the same kind of food: a huge serving of mac and cheese with tuna. He makes as much as we make for the three of us, but wolfs it down himself, gradually exchanging information in between bites. When Venado reveals that we are thru-hiking, the stranger stops eating. "Are you Venado?"

"Yeah!" says Venado, smiling.

The hiker identifies himself as Nature Boy, a veteran thru-hiker who hopes to be the first of the class of 2010 to reach Katahdin.

"I've been following you since down in Pennsylvania. I saw you were planning on getting off in Vermont and I was hoping to catch you before you got there."

"Well you just caught us," I tell him.

"Yeah, catching you guys is what gets me going in the morning."

It turns out he left from Springer Mountain, Georgia, in early January but had to get off the trail because of the snow, and then restart later in the month. He tells us about the south. "Georgia," he says, "they never heard of a switchback; every trail goes straight up and straight down. And if you get lost, just look around for the highest mountain—that's where the trail will be."

His words don't faze us and he relents. "You guys'll be fine," he says. "You got your legs."

He is still in his tent when we leave the next morning, but he catches up with us after a few miles. He stops long enough to say hello and let me take a picture of him and the kids together, and then he leaves us in the proverbial dust.

"Thirty miles a day, he said," I remind the kids. We do eighteen miles a day three days in a row, and considering the size of Venado's legs, that's not bad. The big-mile days bring us rapidly nearer to the Vermont border. Reading one of the registers along the way, Venado finds an entry by Nature Boy. "He says he stopped at the restaurant in Dalton and had two cheeseburgers, two cokes, a large order of fries, a strawberry milkshake, and two huge chocolate chip cookies."

"Read that again," Bluebell says, and we recite his menu again. We too had stopped at the Dalton restaurant, and I had told the kids to order and eat all they could, but we hadn't come anywhere near Nature Boy's appetite.

Along the way through Dalton, a day-hiker had given Bluebell and Venado a half dozen energy bars, flavors they have never tried before, and on top of Mount Greylock, a haunt of Henry David Thoreau and other notables, the kids have an all-out war over who will get the white chocolate macadamia nut one. Venado tosses it away to keep Bluebell from getting it and she punches him.

I roar, "Enough!" and pluck the bar out of the weeds and eat it.

"That's not fair," the kids protest.

"Life is not fair," I remind them, chewing. "Any food you guys fight over is automatically mine."

Venado marches off in angry tears, and in the labyrinth of trails on top of the mountain it takes half an hour to get him back. In the process we meet some other hikers, two clean-cut white guys in their mid-thirties, very straitlaced looking, and I ask if they have seen a little boy. No they haven't. Feeling the palpable tension, they start asking questions: Is everything okay? Are these your kids? Should we call the police?

At last, Venado shows up, and I hustle him and his sister down the trail. "Listen, you guys," I tell them, "not everyone might think taking your kids out hiking the AT is a good idea. If we keep having big fights in public, eventually somebody is going to call the cops and we're going to have to do a lot of explaining. So let's cool it."

We hike on through some patches of snow left under the fir and spruce on the north side of the mountain. It's April 25, so I take a picture of it. "This is probably the last we'll see," I say, but I forget to knock on wood.

We make it to Vermont late in the gray, drizzly afternoon. The trail crosses a muddy road not accounted for in the trail guide, which leaves us wondering if we have passed the shelter. Venado heads back with instructions to go no more than half a mile and blow his whistle if he finds the shelter.

Bluebell and I wait, and by chance a car, headlights and wipers on, comes slithering up the muddy road. The driver stops when we flag him down; he tells us there's another road a half mile further on, and that's probably the one we're looking for. "This is just a road into some camps," he says.

We blow on our whistles impatiently, calling for Venado, and stare down the trail. Finally he comes back, complaining that he couldn't hear us, and we hurry on in the lowering gloom, nearly missing the worn little sign for Seth Warner Lean-to, the seediest wooden box ever deemed a shelter.

In the morning, reading the register, we find a long entry by some folks who finished the Long Trail back in the fall; it lists the things they used, including various fashion magazines and "12 bottles of nail polish, all pink," and things they carried but did not use, such as: "extra socks, freeze-dried food . . ." We can barely read we are laughing so uncontrollably—when you've been on the trail a while, and are worn a bit thin, little things can be hysterical. We'd already been entertained all through Connecticut by "Hannah's Hiking Tips," entries in the register written in colored pens and adorned with stickers of Hannah Montana. The one we repeat often describes how Hannah buys a new headlamp every time hers goes out. "But then this cute guy showed me that it has these things called batteries inside—Wow!" Venado repeats for the umpteenth time, and we all laugh again.

We leave Seth Warner in high spirits, planning to stop in Bennington for a resupply and be back on the trail by late afternoon. Unconcerned by the light morning mist, we don our ponchos but not rain chaps. When the mist thickens slightly, everyone hunkers down to a steady pace. "I don't want to stop and get wetter by opening packs and getting out more rain gear," I say. But when it turns to a cold steady rain, we find ourselves hiking with wet arms and legs, and the chill of the lingering winter works its way into our bodies.

"There's a hut ahead—Congdon," I remind everyone. "But no telling exactly how far."

"Poppy, I'm cold."

"My hands are really cold," says Bluebell.

"Me too, you guys, me too. Let's see if we can get to the hut."

We quicken the pace, but wet as we are, it doesn't warm us up. "Listen, you guys, we have to push hard to stay warm. Nobody can fall down—it's not an option, so don't do it. We can't stop, otherwise we'll have to stop for good, set up the tent, and do the hypothermia drill."

We charge along through the thick spruce forests, dark and dripping wet. Further on, Venado slips in the mud, goes down hard, and comes up hurt, crying. We give him a hug. "Come on. Ten minutes more, and if we don't see the hut, we'll put up the tent," I promise him. "We're in danger of getting hypothermia."

Another hundred yards down the trail, Bluebell, in the lead, calls out, and we see the wet logs and slanting roof of the hut ahead. We tumble in and I give instructions: wet clothes off, dry clothes on, pads and sleeping bags out and zip 'em together, jump into bags.

"I can barely move my fingers," says Bluebell.

"Yeah, I'm fumbling too," I tell her, laughing. "That was close, you guys. That was the most dangerous experience we've had yet."

Venado and Bluebell burrow into the zipped-together bags on one of the hard bunks, and after setting up the stove on the old scarred table nearby, and putting water to boil, I climb in with them. From the comfort of the bags we make hot chocolate, followed by beef stroganoff. Venado and Bluebell wrap cold fingers around hot bowls. "Please do not spill," I remind them. "Remember what your mother said about keeping clean, and think about wild animals. They stay clean; it's part of survival."

After an hour we find ourselves laughing and giggling, even though the rain has turned to heavy snow. "Four point three miles to Bennington, and I think we better get a hotel there," I say.

"Yeah!" says Bluebell, and she is the first out of the bag. "Let's go!"

Dressed in our last dry clothes, and fully geared up for the weather, we set off in high spirits, heading down to the highway that leads to Bennington, Vermont, and a hotel room. The thin layer of snow masks the true state of the trail, and Bluebell plows ankle deep into a mud hole. Venado and I laugh, having misjudged the trail and done the same thing numerous times.

A mile out from the hut, Bluebell stops dead and raises her hand, pointing. We all stop. On the trail ahead, coming towards us, we see our first bear of the trip; it does not see us and blunders along, sniffing here and there at the sides of the path. I watch until it reaches a point where, if it reacted badly to a sudden scare, we would not have much response time. I blow such a loud blast on my whistle that the kids, standing ahead of me, jump; the bear looks up, turns, and hightails it into the woods, disappearing down into a ravine.

"A bear! A bear!" It's the talk of the trail all the way to the road, and beyond. "We saw a bear!"

Wide-eyed and smiling, the kids tell everyone we meet when we hit town.

A bear!

It's still snowing the next day when we get a call to our room at the Crimson Maple Inn. "Checkout time is twelve o'clock," says a woman with a lilting Indian accent. She had given us a box of Ritz crackers the day before, after we had told her we'd been to India, but she obviously wasn't going to give us extra time in that room. We pack up for at the last minute, and pay ten dollars for a shuttle that takes us out of town and drops us at the edge of the wintry woods.

Carrying full packs and some fresh goodies from a butcher shop we'd passed, we wade through a foot of slushy snow, up and up for a mile to Melville Nauheim Shelter. Some older tracks, mostly buried under new snow, make the work a little easier, and we find the shelter occupied by two retired carpenters from Connecticut. "We came up here last night," says one, throwing wood on a big fire they've got going. "This is as far as we got."

By late afternoon the snow tapers off, and the sunset cuts under the clouds, filling the woods with a rich, rosy light. I take out the steaks we brought from town, a much-needed charge of protein. We spear them onto sharpened sticks and lay them on a grate, letting them grill until fat drips sizzling into the fire and the smell demands a taste. I eat the cooked part off mine and put it back on the fire. "Just eat what's cooked," I tell the kids. "And then cook it some more."

"Smells good," says one of our shelter mates.

"It is," I tell him, without offering any. "We need this."

In the morning the carpenters head down the mountain, apparently content to have hiked a mile in and a mile out.

Bluebell, Venado, and I venture out over the unbroken trail, and find it slow going. Plastered onto the trees, the white snow covers the white blazes, and glaring bright under the clear skies, it blankets the woods in an even layer that make the trail difficult to follow. An hour out of camp Venado complains of a headache and pain in his eyes. "It hurts," he says, squinting. "I need to go back."

"Hold on," I say, and offer to make him a snow mask. Using the stiff liner page from Benton MacKaye's book and an extra shoelace, we fashion a slitted mask like the Eskimos use to prevent snow blindness.

The mask may prevent snow blindness, but in the woods it makes Venado virtually blind, and he must slow down to avoid tripping. After two miles heading higher up the mountain, we encounter deeper snow, and Venado is none the better for his mask.

"What do we want to do?" I ask my children.

"Go back," Venado says.

"Doesn't matter to me," says Bluebell.

"Okay, let's go back. We have just enough food to lay over a day and still make it to Story Spring."

Back at the shelter the kids play wild in the snow, and Bluebell builds an April 29 snowman. She and Venado get their boots wet searching for enough wood to keep the fire going to dry their boots. Venado builds a mound of snow in front of the outhouse door.

Late in the day a bunch of young guys arrive and set up their tents in a nearby clearing. They are from a hiking club at some college in Boston.

"Where are you going?" Venado asks.

"Up to the tower on Glastonbury, then back tomorrow," one of them replies.

Venado smiles, and I nod. "These guys'll be breaking trail for us all the way up the mountain," I say to the kids.

Venado has been really into lion traps lately, and he gets onto the subject with the college guys. They agree to dig some pits in the morning, in case there are any lions around.

"That doesn't sound like a promising venture," I say to Venado.

I get up early the next morning with the urgent need of someone who has been eating mushy food for weeks on end. But when I get to the privy I discover that Venado's snow mound has frozen solid in front of the door, and I have to race out into the woods. I wake the kids up. "Venado, before we leave here you better clear that outhouse door or those college guys are going to want a word with you."

We pack up and set off on our own tracks. Crossing a wide clearing—the right-of-way for a power line—we flush out a hen turkey near the edge of the woods. With a great squawk, she rises up big and black, almost in slow motion, her broad wings flapping and scattering snow from the low-hanging branches. Wide-eyed, Venado and his sister watch it, smiling as it vanishes into the white woods. We all stand there for a minute, looking at the place where it went; then turn to each other, mouths agape.

Before we reach the end of the previous day's tracks, the gang from the hiking club passes us and forges ahead. In the high forest full of snow, springs burst frequently from the ground, so the kids and I carry the bare minimum of water, less than a liter each; with the low amount of water and with two days food off our backs, we make good time, staying surprisingly close to the college boys.

At Goddard Shelter, full now with the young men, we decide to go another six miles to Kid Gore, mostly downhill. We climb the fire tower on Glastonbury and enjoy the panoramic view, with snow-covered mountains to the north and south of us and naked sunny valleys off to the east and west.

Footprints on the bridge

"Tomorrow we meet your mom, at around noon."

"Where?"

"At Story Spring. About six miles from Kid Gore, mostly downhill. She's bringing some yummy food."

The next morning we leave Kid Gore and the snow behind and descend toward the warm valley, reaching Story Spring before noon. We find it empty, nobody there with food for us. So we eat what we've got—some energy bars and gorp—and head down toward the road. On a ridge I manage to pick up a cell phone signal; a text comes in bearing a startling message: *Car broke down. I have to deal with this. You're on your own.*

I assume it's her first reaction, and that she'll rent a car and come get us. But when she finally answers her cell phone, she makes it crystal clear. She needs to get a reliable car, pronto, and that's her priority. "This is your thing," she says. "You're going to have to figure out a way home."

The kids, listening to my end of the conversation, stare at me in disbelief, on the verge of tears.

"Is she coming?"

"No."

The tears come, and I hug them both. I take a deep breath. "Come on. We have no food, so we have to do something. Let's get moving."

"What will we do?" asks Bluebell, a note of panic in her voice. Venado echoes her question with equal concern.

"Listen, you guys, your mom has a good reason for what she's doing. She has to work, and she has to take care of herself, and we have to figure something out on our own. Now, just so you know: You couldn't be with a better person than me for a situation like this. I have been in situations like this—and worse—many times: down and out and penniless in strange towns, far from home. Something always works out. We'll be fine."

The shock having passed, I add: "Actually, I think this is really great. Mom is taking care of herself." But I can't get a consensus on that. Besides taking care of herself, she's giving up on being my care-taker, and I realize I'm glad, but I don't get into that.

We reach the road, and by all signs it's the one less traveled. After consulting the guidebook, we start hiking toward Stratton, and a highway. The sun comes out and we have gone from winter to summer in a day. "We'll see if we can get to Brattleboro and get a bus or a train out of there." But every car that passes us on that hot dusty road is headed the other way, and every time we hear something coming up behind us it turns out to be a motorcycle.

"The only thing that comes our way is motorcycles," says Venado. "Suppose we don't get a ride?"

"Listen, we are right where we are supposed to be," I reassure him. "The reason we're not getting a ride now is so that we'll be in the right place at the right time for the perfect ride." And it's prophetically true. We stop to filter water, and I barely get a liter full when an older couple pulls over and offers us a ride to civilization. "You must be on the Appalachian Trail," the woman at the wheel says. Her husband, in the passenger seat, turns to smile at the kids.

"You kids having a good time?"

"Not exactly."

I explain the situation, glossing it over a bit, and the couple shares what they know about hotels on the way to Brattleboro, and busses from there to Boston. They drop us by the side of a road leading to Brattleboro and we start to hitchhike as the sun slides lower in the sky.

"Man, you guys, when we're near the trail we have some legitimacy as hikers, out here we're just homeless." The kids laugh.

"Did you see the way that lady was looking at us?" asks Venado as a car goes by with a gray haired woman frowning through the window at him.

"Geez, if you don't like seeing us out here, pick us up," says his sister. Standing out in front of an antique store where we have gotten water and lots of sympathy, I coach the kids in the art of hitchhiking. "Get in front of me, stand where they can see you. Don't throw things, Venado."

It's all fun until the sun gets close to the mountains and starts turning orange. "This calls for extreme measures," I tell the kids. "We must use the lucky pebble trick." I look around at my feet until I spot a distinctive pebble. "First, you find the lucky pebble and put it in your back left-hand pocket, and you'll get a ride quick. But you have to make sure to take it out of your pocket and throw it as far as you can once you get out of the car."

I'm still telling stories about places where I had used the lucky pebble trick when a little car full of luggage and guitars pulls over. A skinny, high-energy guy, about my age, jumps out. "Okay, this is going to take some rearranging," he says.

We work it out, and squeeze in. "Where you going?" he asks as we get under way.

"Brattleboro."

"That's where I live," he tells us, and introduces himself as Breeze, just Breeze. "I saw you guys there," he says, "and I thought, okay, there's something going on here. I had to pick you up." He turns out to be our angel, and by the time we reach Brattleboro we've been invited to stay at his place with his girlfriend, Robin. Arriving at their big frame house, we meet Robin, a smiling woman with thick dark hair and an easy way about her, which comes in handy when your partner spontaneously decides to bring a bunch of barbarians to your home. It seems okay with her, and we all go to dinner at an outdoor restaurant overlooking the river that runs through town. The kids and I wolf down our food and, as usual, crave more.

"We can't afford it," I say when Venado asks for another sandwich.

I call home. Bluebell and Venado take turns talking to their mom, and she agrees to pick us up in Brattleboro the next morning. She's got a car: a brand new Honda Fit, black.

"Black?" I ask, somewhat incredulous, recalling her first Honda, all hippie painted with moons and stars. Silence on the other end of the line lets me know I'm on thin ice. "I like it," I tell her.

Next morning she arrives around nine. Breeze and Robin have cooked a big breakfast. They share their own experiences of relationship difficulties and play the role of marriage counselors in an obviously fragile situation. Many hugs go round, and invitations to visit again as we bid goodbye to the newest extension of our hiking family.

After getting onto the highway home, we begin negotiations around the big question: Will the hike go on? The discussion goes round and round until the solids settle. Venado definitely wants to take the train south and continue with the plan; Bluebell wants to go home. I claim ambivalence: My feet hurt and my nerves are frayed after three weeks negotiating the trail with two sometimes-squabbling children.

Their mom wants recognition that she fulfilled her commitment to two months support, and carrying us emotionally in many ways. She tells us she will no longer take care of resupply.

Before my wife had arrived, Breeze had advised me to do her a favor and end the hike. But when she'd left us out on the road the day before, it had dramatically changed things. This no-nonsense, sink-or-swim, decisive woman reminds me of the one I'd fallen in love with fifteen years before. Her actions make a statement that I am not responsible for her happiness—she has power over her own life, and if anything can make me fall in love with her again, that is it.

I know in that moment that I am staying with her, and I am hoping she hasn't given up on me. And though I am unable to say it out loud, I feel ninety-nine percent sure that the hike will go on. Venado, I suspect, is a hundred percent sure.

After a long final consultation at the rest stop off I-95 in New Hampshire, Venado's desire to keep hiking tips the scale. Rather than go south, Bluebell agrees to take over putting together and sending resupply boxes, and my wife agrees to give her blessings, and continuing financial support, to the project.

"Are you happy?" she asks as we head for the Greyhound station in Portsmouth.

I shrug. "My feet hurt. I might have been relieved to have called it good enough."

But it's too late to quit. Phase one complete, Venado and I catch a bus out of Portsmouth and sleep that night at a friend's house in Boston. We go to bed wrapped in the excitement and promise of leaving tomorrow, taking the train to Atlanta—the South—another world.

7

MIDNIGHT TRAIN TO GEORGIA

Train riding gives us a much-needed rest. We devour hot dogs from the café car, along with the donuts, chips, fresh fruit, and gorp we've brought along. As the train rolls through D.C. at the end of the day, we spot the Washington Monument illuminated in the last rays of the sun.

"And there's the Smithsonian Institute," I tell Venado, pointing to an array of ornate buildings.

"Can we go there?"

"Not this time, maybe on the way back," I tell him and we drift off to sleep as the train rumbles through the night, carrying us deep into the south.

We wake up the next morning in summertime. Forests rise up the hills that flank the train, and a million new leaves undulating on the soft breeze wave us a welcome as we roll into Georgia. "Now we're in the Appa-lah-chins," says Venado, pronouncing it the southern way, and smiling at the thousand shades of green. He wants to have breakfast in the moving restaurant, the dining car, and I'd promised him one onboard meal, so we totter down there, weaving with the rattle and lurch of the cars, and share a table with a dignified older man named Charles. He's heading to Georgia to visit family, he tells us, and at the table he displays impeccable manners. When he puts his napkin in his lap, I do the same and nudge Venado, mouthing the word "napkin."

After a fine breakfast of French toast on a sunny morning, we arrive in Atlanta. We're couch surfing again and our host, Kimbi, meets us at the train station and takes us to her house on the outskirts of the city. Her husband's brother has offered to take us to the trailhead the next day, and so we have time to kill.

"You could go to the aquarium. It's brand new," Kimbi says, and she offers us the use of her car. But I say the aquarium might be over-stimulating, even on a Tuesday. "We've been out in the woods a long time." We opt to go to the Botanical Garden. What else would hikers of the forest do when not hiking in the forest? "It seems like it would be quieter," I suggest. "Besides, it's closer, and I haven't driven a car since last September, let alone in a strange city."

"Do you want me to drive you?" she asks.

"That might be a good idea."

We hope to familiarize ourselves with the local flora at the Botanical Garden, but the Atlanteans already know about their own flora and have filled their garden with exotic plants from all over the world. Still, Venado and I enjoy the greenhouses full of flowers and frogs, especially one with a covey of quail wandering around under the dense plants in something akin to a natural setting.

The next morning we have our bags packed and sit with them out in front of the house, waiting for Kimbi's brother-in-law to pick us up. He arrives on time, and on the way out of Atlanta we pick up two bottles of HEET stove fuel at a BP station. For the first time we hear the news about the oil spill in the Gulf of Mexico; it's worse than anyone thought.

"Are you going to write about it?" a friend asks me in an email.

"I don't think it would be good for my mental health," I reply.

At Amicalola Falls, the start of the approach trail to Springer Mountain and the Appalachian Trail, we weigh our packs: twenty-six and thirteen pounds, respectively—impressive, coming out of the gate with five days' food and two liters of water each. Venado leads the way into the woods again, and it's a whole new game. We're in Georgia and it is lush and green, the dirt is red, the rhododendrons thick and filled with many more birds than we saw in the north. In our first few miles we see a black-throated blue warbler, an ovenbird, and a scarlet tanager, all very close. We start to meet a new type of centipede. Venado spots it the first time—it's black with yellow legs and yellow spots down its back—and soon we see them fairly often. Suffice it to say that the journey from the snow and just-awakening forests of the north to the fully awakened southern Appalachians has awakened us.

And we are traveling much lighter. I wear a pair of hand-me-down Merrell trail runners; Venado has on a pair of Teva sandals. Between us we have one sleeping bag and a five-by-six-foot polar fleece blanket, Venado's Ensolite pad, and my self-inflating Thermarest pad—a concession to comfort. We have our lightweight ponchos and leggings, shorts, quick-dry pants, and a one-person tent. We saunter up the smooth red clay trail to Springer Mountain, making such good time it surprises us when we get to the top. At the summit a bronze plaque, imbedded into a rock, depicts the figure of an old-fashioned hiker climbing a hill. "Appalachian Trail, Georgia to Maine. A footpath for those who seek fellowship with the wilderness," reads the inscription.

The first person we meet is Galilee Man, a fifty-five-year-old Israeli all pumped up to set a speed record for the trail. "Forty days," he says. We note that while it is May 5, Galilee Man has postdated his entry in the rgister to May 7, so he's already two days ahead of schedule. He says his pack weighs a hefty forty pounds.

"Why is it so heavy?" Venado asks.

"Vitamins," Galilee Man says.

I raise an eyebrow at that one. "Vitamins or steroids?" I wonder later.

"Poppy, what are ster . . . "

"Never mind."

Later in the night, Venado shifts around next to me.

"Are you awake?" I ask.

"Yeah, I keep thinking about all the stuff we saw today."

"Yeah, me too."

"It's all so different."

With more than six hundred miles on our legs, the flat, clear trail poses no difficulties for us, and right away we begin passing the late starters.

The greenhorns who provided a great source of comic fodder for writer Bill Bryson in his book *A Walk in the Woods* prove to be a great source of extra food for us.

We hike three miles out of Springer and arrive at a shelter to find another father and son team just waking up.

"That was a long climb yesterday," says the father. "I think our packs are too heavy."

Venado and I look over their extensive pile of food and gear, and nod.

"You guys need any food?" he asks.

"What have you got?" I ask back.

It turns out they have a month's supply of powdered vitamin C drinks—I relieve them of twelve packets, each good for a liter. Venado deigns to take a half dozen energy bars. But we refuse the Mountain House freeze-dried dinners, and they jam them into their huge packs.

We stash our booty in our food bags and sit down to breakfast, watching the still heavily laden father and son head up the trail. An hour later we catch up with them near the summit of a steep mountain.

"I suppose it would be a bit shabby to ask for one of those Mountain House dinners now that they've carried them up the mountain for us," I whisper. Venado shrugs, and we let it go.

Later on that crisp morning, with a light breeze dancing among the leaves of the trees, we come to the place where the Benton MacKaye and Appalachian Trails part. "Might be fitting, in honor of MacKaye's inspiration for us," I say, looking down the path blazed with white triangles. "It's a little longer than if we stick with the AT."

The Benton MacKaye Trail, besides honoring MacKaye, is intended to reduce pressure on the earliest miles of the Appalachian Trail, where thousands of aspiring thru-hikers start off and often realize they are not ready to go all the way. I'm tempted to take this less-traveled path, but there is another consideration.

"We're purists," says Venado, pointing to the familiar white blazes that mark the AT. He has to stick with the white blazes, and I have to stick with him, so MacKaye comes with us instead. We talk about him often; whenever we tell anyone about our Facebook page, "The Barbarian Utopia," we have to provide some background for the outrageous name. We have to put those words in the mouth of the trail's very cultured visionary, and explain them against any anti-Barbarian predispositions. Most people we meet have never heard of MacKaye, other than that he has a trail named after him, and who knows why? We do our best to share the Utopian vision with them, but we too had come to the wilderness with misconceptions.

Clothing and food lie scattered all along the early miles of the trail. "These folks must've read *A Walk in the Woods*," I say, "where those guys litter their stuff all over the place." We find the next shelter full of all sorts of gear.

"Look at all this stuff, Poppy!"

"Yeah, you could get just about everything you need here, including nail clippers," I say, picking up a pair. "This is fortuitous." I trim my fingers and take my boots off to do my toes. Venado cuts his nails too, and puts the clippers back in the shelter.

Getting ready to leave, I hold a small lightweight pillow in my hand, considering it for a long time before tossing it back into a corner full of sleeping bags, tents, flashlights, and other precious items. Venado looks longingly at a snazzy water bottle, but it's heavy. In the end we take only a map, good to Fontana Dam.

Late on our third night, just at dark, we hustle down off Blood Mountain and into Neels Gap, where the trail passes through a building that houses an outfitter on one side and a hostel on the other.

"Poppy, why did we have to come here?"

"What, you wanted to stay up there with the bear?"

"Yeah."

"Well we can't afford to lose our food to a bear. Besides, that shelter was crowded."

We have come off Blood Mountain, the site of a famous battle between the Cherokee and Creek tribes in the days before European incursions, and now the site of a six-hundred-pound bear that has figured out how to cut food bags out of the trees.

"He was here last night," a ranger up on the mountain had told us. "People were shouting and throwing rocks, but he just went through the bags like there was nobody there." As the ranger talked about the bear, a hiker had come out of the shelter with a long bowie knife tied to a shaft of wood like a spear. "It's not going to get my food," he'd said, and that convinced me we needed to move on.

"This could turn into a real circus, Venado. Let's go." Venado resisted, but when I had threatened to leave him up there, he'd given up.

It's worth the sacrifice. In the kitchen of the Neels Gap Hostel we find a big wood stove surrounded by treasure troves of gear and food, everything imaginable, left behind by overloaded or defeated hikers.

"Look at all these boots," I say.

"Those are for people who need them," says a heavyset hiker sitting in a recliner.

Venado and I drink tea and hot chocolate, eat cookies from the hiker box, and take showers. Refreshed, we head out into the woods and camp for free. Next morning we're back at the hostel kitchen, raiding the food box for goodies and sugar.

"That's for thru-hikers," says the frowning man from the night before.

"We *are* thru-hikers."

The man bends down and looks Venado straight in the eye. "Are you a thru-hiker?"

"Georgia to Maine," responds Venado, with pure innocence, and he returns to rifling one of the gear boxes. "Here's a belt!" he says holding up a web belt with a plastic snap.

"Yeah, that's perfect for you," I tell him.

When the outfitters open up later in the morning we go in and buy some energy bars and fuel. Venado strikes up a conversation with one of the workers, who gives him some fishing line and a dry fly.

"What was that guy's name?" I ask after we leave.

"Lumpy," Venado says, and follows up quickly with: "Poppy, can we go fishing?"

"Sure, we'll see. We're not really equipped to deal with fish, and I don't want to get all smelly in bear country, but let's see what happens."

We're on the subject of fish now—sample questions:

Is it easy to catch a trout? (Depends on how hungry they are.) How big do trout get? (Depends on the species and environment.) Why didn't the trout live in our pond? (Because the cormorants and

Lumpy gives Venado some fishing gear

kingfishers ate them.) What other fish can we put in our pond? (All kinds: carp, bass, sunfish.) What's the biggest fish we can put in our pond? (A Mekong catfish.) How big do they get? (Big enough to eat a goat.) Can you go bass fishing with a lobster boat? (Yes.) What's the biggest fish you can catch with a lobster boat? (Bluefin tuna, maybe.)

We make good time on the smooth trail out of Neels Gap, hiking through hardwood forests, and passing a waterfall where Venado tosses sticks in and watches them disappear. We spend a cold night at Low Gap, then blast out of there before dawn, hiking a fast seven miles before stopping for lunch at Blue Mountain Shelter. We find a small group of long-haired boys lounging around the shelter, eating a late breakfast. "We're boy scouts," one of them tells us.

"Really?" we say, almost in unison.

One of the scoutmasters, a woman, says they're out for the weekend and plan to finish their hike at the road a few miles north; she offers Venado some snacks, and me a cup of coffee.

Another of the scoutmasters gives us peanut butter in a tube, and when I squeeze some into a bowl it looks like a soft brown turd. I tip up the bowl and show it to Venado. His jaw drops. "No, it's not what you think," I tell him. "We're going to eat it." I squeeze jelly on top, and crumble our broken crackers into the bowl; then I mix it all up and we eat it with our spoons, passing the bowl back and forth as we try to swallow the sticky glop.

"It's good."

Venado agrees.

An Appalachian Trail ridge-runner, a hiker paid to hike and look after a specific section of the trail, rolls in from the north and sits down with us, unpacking his lunch from a small daypack. His name is Razor, and when the subject of Benton MacKaye comes up, as it often does with us, he talks about the feud between MacKaye and Myron Avery, the no-nonsense naval lawyer who got the trail built and was the first to hike every mile of it.

The pragmatic Avery had had a very different vision of the trail, one far less philosophical than MacKaye's. The two had fought over what wilderness meant, and when the FDR administration proposed building highways along the ridgelines, Myron Avery had agreed to the plan.

"They hated each other," Razor tells us. "After they built the Blue Ridge Parkway, MacKaye washed his hands of the whole thing and went off and started the Wilderness Society," he says. "He never got involved in the AT again till after Myron Avery died." We found out later that Razor's version of the story had the chronology a bit mixed up, but he captured the essence of the events.

"Avery grew up in Lubec, Maine, about twenty-three miles from where we live," I tell the ridge-runner. "But we're more tuned in to MacKaye and his vision of the trail as a Utopia. I've got a good idea of the kinda guy Avery was," I say. "Hard work and pragmatism is the way of the Down-easter. I'm not surprised that for him some wilderness was expendable."

Later that day we pick up a resupply box and fuel at a camp just off the trail on the road leading to Hiawassee. Bluebell has put a bag of chocolate chip cookies in with the usual stuff.

"You want to carry these cookies?" I ask Venado.

"No."

"We better eat 'em."

And in the time it takes us to pack up our food, the cookies vanish. A guy getting off the trail takes our trash away and we hike on into an easterly breeze that delivers rain for the next three days. Along the way we meet many aspiring thru-hikers. At Plum Orchard Gap Shelter, one of the fanciest shelters we have seen since Peters Mountain, a tall, lanky hiker arrives carrying two big fat sticks for hiking poles. He introduces himself to us as "Clark."

"No trail name?" we ask.

"Not yet."

The next morning I get up to record a wood thrush singing in the first faint light of a new day. I listen to its flutelike music for a few minutes before waking Venado and making our customary early departure.

"Do you think those girls are going to make it?" Venado asks the next day when we leave another shelter occupied by two young women from New Hampshire.

"You can never tell. There's no guarantee for anybody. I've heard of people quitting in the 100-Mile Wilderness. We may not make it."

"Yeah, but they are still sleeping and their stuff is all wet."

"Sure, they don't seem very motivated or organized, but we'll see."

Aside from one skinny guy who had passed us on the first day, most of the people we meet during our first week in the South vanish behind us for good. Even Galilee Man disappears from the shelter registers eventually. But on our eighth day in the south we stop at a shelter for lunch and meet Cowboy. He's not thru-hiking, but aside from a heavy suede cowboy hat, his gear and the way he moves say he's a hiker. "We already did six hundred miles from Harpers Ferry to Vermont," Venado tells him, and then has to explain the whole hiking plan.

"I'm just going as far as Hot Springs," says Cowboy.

Venado nods in a way much more grown-up than I'd seen before. "The fog came into the shelter last night and got everything wet," he tells Cowboy. "And there were these girls there who had all their stuff out and it was all wet."

"We were very fortunate to have put up our tent in the shelter," I say. "But it's all wet."

"Well, I think it's starting to clear up now," says Cowboy, packing up to go. He takes off ahead of us, and when we reach our goal for the day and find the shelter empty, Venado urges me to hike on to the next one.

"It's five miles, Venado. Do you think we can make it?"

"It's mostly downhill. We can make it."

"Okay." And we hike on to Rock Gap Shelter, just south of Franklin, North Carolina. In the last hour of the day we hear loud voices and look down from the trail at a shelter in the hollow; its eaves are festooned with bright-colored gear, and people spill out all around it. Being purists, Venado and I hike to the northern entrance and back-track to the shelter, where the other hikers greet us warmly. Cowboy has staked out his tent on some level ground and we pitch ours nearby. He has a bear cable set up, and he tells us we can hang our food bags with his. While Venado sets up the tent, I go back to the crowded shelter where we have left our evening's food and cooking gear piled on an open end of the table. The other hikers direct me to the water source and I am delighted to find a piped spring. A hundred yards above it sits the privy, but I hope for the best and fill the bottles without breaking out the filter.

Venado joins me back at the picnic table and amidst a thousand questions back and forth we explain our mission and learn that we have finally fallen in with a group of real hikers, people with sensible gear and trail names: Buffer, Hot Wing, and Georgia Trail Dog. None are committed to walking all the way to Katahdin, but, like Cowboy, they expect to go some distance. We tell them stories from up north and recite "the litany" for them, rattling off the names of every campsite we have stayed at so far, from Ed Garvey back in Maryland to Rock Gap where we have just arrived.

"That's impressive," says Buffer. "I can't even remember the name of where I stayed last night."

When morning comes we all prepare to hike together. Most of us plan to go in to Franklin, where Venado and I hope to find a resupply box waiting.

We hit a snag getting out of camp. Cowboy has used a distinctive moosehead-shaped carabiner to hook his bear cable to an eyebolt in a tree, but the odd shape makes it impossible to unhook. He cuts the bear cable free and leaves his carabiner hanging from the eyebolt.

Once on the trail Venado and I take the lead with Georgia Trail Dog, a local character who knows all there is to know about the flora, fauna, and history of the area. "I ain't smelt a polecat the whole time I been out here," he says, and Venado asks what a "polecat" is.

"I think you call it a skunk," says Georgia Trail Dog. He goes on to show us wild azaleas, and tells us stories about the Cherokee and the old days during the Civil War when his great great granddaddy rode these hills looking for Yankees and deserters. "If they didn't like the flag you were flying they wouldn't take kindly to it. They took one fellow out and hung him." Venado pummels him with questions that the garrulous Trail Dog answers at length, glad for an eager listener in a scattershot conversation.

"Lots of people up here were for the North," Trail Dog says. "They don't call this 'Union County' for nothing."

The lean, balding Trail Dog works as a gardener at an Atlanta country club, he tells us. "But whenever I can, I come out here. I don't mind the heat down there—it's just the humidity I don't like."

The rest of the crew, who have been with Trail Dog for several days, let on that they are glad to not have to listen to his stories anymore. "It's just that he's so *loud*," says one. But we love him; he's the kind of guy who has the information we want.

Five miles out, the trail drops down to a highway, Trail Dog leaves us. "This is as afar as I go," he says. "I like to stay in the country I know."

Venado and I join the rest of the town-bound hikers in the back of a pickup heading into Franklin. We pick up another resupply box at the post office, but, having gotten ahead of schedule, we don't need all of it. We give a pile of food to Hot Wing, who earned his name by eating a pile of spicy chicken wings in Hiawassee. "It was free if you could eat it all and keep it down," he says. "It wasn't worth it, though. I got really sick." He feels better now, but having started his hike on a whim he's still desperate to get food anyway he can, and his eyes light up when he sees the mac and cheese dinners, energy bars, and dried fruit we offer him.

Around midafternoon we leave Buffer and Hot Wing at a motel in Franklin and head back to the mountains, making a steep climb up to Siler Bald Shelter, where we meet two thru-hikers, Spoon and Popeye, who had been hiking with Buffer and Hot Wing. "I had to get away from Georgia Trail Dog," says Popeye, shaking his head.

As Popeye, a recently unemployed stockbroker, and I dive into a discussion of global economics fueled by MacKaye's philosophy, Venado finds a spot for the tent, and sets it up all by himself. When I see the lay of the site I express some skepticism, but it's late, and we're tired. All through the night I have to keep rolling Venado up the hill. Finally, I switch sides and a little while later he wakes up and pushes me uphill. "You're squishing me."

"I'm not the one who set up the tent on a sliding board. Be a little more selective next time." I roll away, and Venado giggles.

"I didn't set it up on a sliding board."

"Hmmpff."

As we hike along, Venado shows me the star-shaped leaf of the sweet gum. "Georgia Trail Dog said sweet gum is good for making an Indian toothbrush," he says. "Except he calls it a mountain toothbrush." Venado tells me about how Trail Dog makes bows and arrows, carving the bows from yew. "He said you can glue sinew along the back to make it stronger. What's sinew?"

"Not much, what's sinew with you?"

"Poppy!"

Often as we hike through the damp woods, I stop to photograph wildflowers, the ephemerals, and we post the pictures on our Facebook page so people can tell us what they are. Laurie Potteiger from the Appalachian Trail Conservancy helps us identify trout lilies and various trilliums; another, we learn from Venado's mom, is an orchid—lady's slipper.

Aside from a some killer hills, like one that goes up eight hundred feet in half a mile, the trail runs smooth underfoot, and springs erupt all over the mountainsides. At one point we find a spot where the water boils up through a bed of sand.

"That must be really good water," I venture.

"Yeah," Venado agrees. "It's getting all cleaned by the sand."

At lunchtime we meet a pair of octogenarians who tell us their shared trail name is the Pink Panthers. As we unpack our lunches at a scenic overlook, they appear to be eating the same sort of homemade trail food we often do, and we ask about it. "We prepare everything ourselves ahead of time," says Mrs. Panther.

"Well, it looks like it's done you well if you're still out here," I say to the thin and muscular couple. "How far are you going?"

"Oh, we don't know. Home to New York maybe," Mrs. Panther says.

"We thru-hiked in ninety-six," says Mr. Panther, "and when Mrs. Panther was coming up on her eightieth birthday, I asked, what do you want to do? She said, 'let's go back on the trail.' So here we are." I ask them to flank Venado for a photo.

"The oldest and the youngest—eight to eighty."

"Are you going to the Nantahala Outdoor Center?" Venado wants to know.

"The NOC?"

"Yeah," says Venado learning to call our destination by the literal pronunciation of its acronym—the "knock."

"We just go as far as we can, we don't have a schedule," they tell him.

"Do you know if they have Wi-Fi at the NOC?" I ask.

"I think so," says Mrs. Panther.

"Oh no," Venado says, looking at me and shaking his head. He imitates me hunched over my iPhone squinting and tapping madly on the little keys.

"I gotta cover the basics, my son. I won't be on it that much."

After a hot and sweaty afternoon hike we arrive at Cold Spring Shelter. We find the aptly named spring and take turns using our cook pot to dump icy cold water all over ourselves; it takes our breath away.

"Oh man, that feels great."

But it's a dump of a shelter, with a dirty, wet sleeping bag lying on the ground outside, and walls covered with nasty graffiti. Even a local scoutmaster who shows up tosses an aluminum tuna packet into the fire pit, already strewn with unburnable garbage. The seedy shelter fills up fast with overnight hikers, including the Panthers.

"This doesn't look like it's going to be very comfortable," I say quietly to Venado. When Spoon and Popeye show up, we all opt to camp on a ridge above the shelter. Later, the scoutmaster joins us around a fire we've made and regales us with stories of his hillbilly father. "He called a spring a 'sprang.' He had all kinds of things like that." The scoutmaster says his troop is planning to put on a feed for hikers the following week, and he tells how the kids had gone around requesting food from local stores and would serve it up trailside. "Course you fellers'll be long gone by then."

"Yeah."

Eager to get to the NOC, Venado and I hit the trail before anyone else wakes up. We arrive in the midafternoon at a wilderness playground, replete with restaurants, a hostel, outfitters, kayak and raft rentals, and campuswide Wi-Fi. The rest of the crew dribbles in all afternoon and evening, along with a few new faces in our thru-hiker family, Johnny Walker and Flip Flop, who has gained a reputation up and down the trail as the guy who arrived at Springer Mountain in a pair of flip-flops and carrying a school backpack. By the time Flip Flop got past Neels Gap, however, he was booted up and carrying some impressive gear, all free.

As we finagle free showers and dump six people's worth of clothes into a washing machine to save a dollar, various hikers make runs to the general store for more and more beer until everyone—except Venado and I—has a good buzz going. A slender twenty-something woman in short shorts and a tank top comes down from the group dining room. She explains that she's a girl scout leader and her troop has cooked more food than they can eat. Do we thru-hikers want some hamburgers and hot dogs?

Of course, we do.

It's a race, and being sober, Venado and I have an edge. First into the kitchen, we get a hamburger and a hot dog each, while latecomers to the feast make do with spaghetti sandwiches—a novel invention. We all watch painfully as girl scouts walk by and toss barely touched burgers into the garbage.

The scout leader comes into the kitchen and looks around at nine trail-toughened, bearded men. "I'm looking for . . . " Everyone except Venado looks intently at her. "A big . . . " She's turning around the room slowly with her hand up as if grasping something, looking for the word. (A big what?) "Spoon."

"Uh, I think there's one over here," says one of the hikers, and holds up a spoon. She snags it and leaves.

"Man, I did not know where that was going," somebody says.

"I'm wondering what she made of that," I reply.

"Made of what?" Venado asks, but nobody answers.

We polish off all the food and disperse. Popeye and Spoon have bunks in a four-bed room.

"There's nobody but us in there," Popeye says. "You guys are welcome to stay."

I tell him thanks but I want to get Venado out of this environment. "Come on, Venado," I say and we head out into the woods. But steady rain and steep, rough ground make it hard to find a camping site. As darkness falls we turn round and retreat to the hostel. We make a deal to take a zero day, pay for the room the next night, and let Popeye and Spoon crash for free.

Next morning Venado wants to do a river trip, and he refuses to take no for an answer.

"It costs forty dollars!" I protest.

"So?"

We watch rafts and kayaks come down the river, the kayakers in bright outfits spinning and playing in the standing waves of the rapids. We wander over to get the information, but I have trouble committing. "I don't know, Venado—this looks like a real budget buster."

"Poppy, we have to do it." And it seems we do.

The woman behind the counter at the raft rental place explains all the options—group raft with guide, group raft without guide, two-person raft unguided, double ducky (an inflatable kayak), and so on. We decide to rent a two-person raft, unguided, for the two o'clock run. "Does he weigh sixty pounds?" The woman wants to know. "He has to be sixty pounds to go unguided in a raft."

"Yeah, he's sixty pounds," I assure her—at least he was when we started.

"Be here at one-thirty so we can get you outfitted and show you the safety video," she tells us.

Popeye decides to accompany us in a single ducky, and at one-thirty we file into a little room with the other rafters and watch the video. I turn and raise my eyebrows at Venado when they talk about what to do if you get thrown from a raft: to float with your feet up and pointed downstream. The video shows lots of images of people getting thrown from rafts. "The last rapid is a class IV rapid," we're told. "Make sure you enter it in the center, stay away from the left. . . "

"If we hit rough water, my boy, stay low," I tell Venado as we choose life jackets, neoprene booties, and paddles and head outside.

"This'll be your raft," one of the guides says. Venado and I look at the hard-bottom yellow raft and nod our approval. The guide and another worker toss it onto a trailer with the other rafts and duckies, and we climb aboard a bus for the ride upstream.

"Watch out for that big rock called 'Jaws,'" says one of the guides. "They got a big sign there." He looks at us. "They don't give rocks around here names like 'Butterfly Kiss,' or 'Cottonball.'"

At the put-in the guides give us our raft and point to the water a hundred yards away. The raft weighs more than we can lift, but Popeye carries his ducky down to the rivers edge and comes back to help. The first rapid, we've been warned, is a class III, and once in the water, Venado paddles hard towards it.

"Easy," I say. "When we hit this, bring your paddle in and get down."

The water grabs us and sucks us toward a standing wave; we smash through it and water explodes over the raft, soaking us. Venado, crouching behind the sturdy air-filled rim of the raft, turns to look at me with a big smile, his hair plastered to his head. I work my paddle from one side to the other in a concentrated effort to maintain some control over the raft, and moments later the rapid spits us out into calm water. After a few more rapids I let Venado help paddle through.

"You like it?" I ask.

"Yeah!"

"That safety video got me worried," I tell him. "But I guess as much time as I've spent on boats, it's only natural I'd get this figured out."

It starts raining again, and we paddle to stay warm, playing tag with Popeye all along the way—Venado chattering excitedly to him whenever we get close.

Whitewater rafting

Approaching the class IV rapid, we draw near to a guided group raft. "How do you go through this?" I ask the guide.

"You come in on the left and then paddle across so you hit in the middle. Just follow us." The guide has a familiar accent.

"Where are you from?" Venado asks.

"Maine." We laugh and trade info about where we live in Maine and how we all ended up on the Nantahala.

"You'll be okay," the guide says as his clients demand his attention.

We follow the guide into the rapid as he told us, and paddle hard for the middle. It's close—the river takes hold of us, and though we get through the first drop okay it spins us round and sends us over the second plunging backwards. Venado braces himself on the floor; I look over my shoulder as the raft tips at a steeper angle, totally out of our control. It looks like we're about to roll, but the raft splashes down flat again. Venado looks up. We're through. We've done it. We paddle hard for the beach, as instructed. "The next rapid is a class V," the guide had told us. "You don't want to go there."

On the beach, we watch Popeye shoot the final rapid with style—arms lifted, holding his paddle triumphantly over his head.

The NOC has a camera set up at the last rapid that automatically takes a picture of everyone who goes through, and then the rafters can buy a print or digital image if they want. Popeye's comes out great, but ours shows my back and a dark spot in the bow that is Venado crouched down and—you'd have to have been there to know it—laughing. We leave the pic and keep the memory.

"I can still feel it," says Venado, getting his land legs back.

"Man, I had all these images of you getting blasted out of the raft, turning upside down, and other catastrophes," I say to him. "But it wasn't so bad."

It rains all night, battering the roof of our room until just before dawn. Heading out after breakfast, we meet the Panthers in the parking lot. Mr. Panther has twisted his knee and they want to go back to Franklin to rest it. Venado shakes hands goodbye with them and leads the way up out of the gorge. On a ridge, he turns to look along the river.

"What?" I ask.

"This is where I want to live."

"It's not bad."

For a week afterwards our talk centers on whitewater rafting. "What's the difference between a whitewater kayak and a sea kayak?" Venado wants to know. "How much does it cost? Would you let me go down the rapids on the East Machias River?" he asks. "How old would I have to be to go down Bad Little Falls in a kayak?"

"Bad Little Falls, back home? Where the water blasts through jagged rocks at a million miles an hour?"

"Yeah."

I look at him. "Twenty-one. And by then I hope you'd know better."

8

WATERSHEDS

"As a rough and ready rule, subject to very liberal modification, the basic seat of geotechnic development [Governance] is the river basin, or watershed, which is a cross section of the land from top summit to ocean level."
—Benton MacKaye, "Folkland as Nation Maker," 1951

Before leaving the NOC, I read from MacKaye's book: "Here then was a marked defect of the original plan. The state, as devised in the Ordinance of 1787, was not a natural unit of growth or sovereignty." The Panthers and a few other passing hikers stand in the parking lot, listening. "MacKaye wanted states to be established around watersheds," I explain, "not arbitrary boundaries. He felt the founding fathers goofed on that, leaving a complex array of separate governments to manage watersheds. He said what we need is watershed-wide governance if we want to control pollution and resource use."

Makes sense, the Panthers agree, as I wrap a rubber band around the unbound pages of MacKaye's book and jam them into the top compartment of my pack. I had paid six dollars on Amazon for the collection of MacKaye's articles and torn the cover off to save weight and space—unaware that the next-cheapest copy was selling for more than seventy dollars.

We make quick time to Fontana and spend the night at a crowded, waterless shelter that sits, oddly enough, on the edge of a reservoir. A tarnished spigot pokes out of a nearby building, but when Venado opens the valve, nothing comes out but air. Desperate, we find a spot free of scum and old tires along the shore of the reservoir and filter a liter of water.

The lengthening days afford us more opportunities to hang out with our shelter mates, and I get into a conversation with a guy named Gary Bassett. It doesn't take us long to realize we are on opposite ends of the political spectrum. But looking out at the man-made lake full of the refuse of Bryson City, North Carolina—all on its way to the Tennessee River and beyond—we find common ground on one theme: that we need to protect our resources from imminent destruction.

In the morning Venado and I cross the Fontana Dam, me walking along with the guidebook open in my hand. "Says here that this is the highest dam in the east."

Venado wants to go down to the bottom, but I say no way. We look over the edge at the massive white concrete wall. "Says this is the Little Tennessee River. It goes all the way to the Ohio, Mississippi, and the Gulf of Mexico."

"Can we get water here?"

"Doesn't look like it. There's a spring five miles up; we'll just sip on what we've got and change it out there."

Often carrying only one liter of water each, we talk every day of where water will be, how pure it is, whether we should filter or not. On the way up to Mollies Ridge we stop at a campground where clear water flows from a piped spring, and we eat a late breakfast in the company of a young buck deer.

"Poppy, look how close he's coming."

"He's pretty tame, isn't he?"

The deer meanders along the meandering stream, nibbling at leaves, ignoring Venado and me.

At Mollies Ridge we meet more tame wildlife: a four-hundred-pound bear, much less welcome than the deer. It forages in the underbrush fifty yards away from us as our scattered family of thru-hikers collects near the shelter. Everyone stands close together, watching.

I look at Venado. "Get over by that tree and be ready to climb."

But Good-to-Go, a new arrival to our loose-knit clan, grabs his camera and charges toward the bear. Everyone expects him to get mauled, and we express some surprise when the bear retreats.

"Damn, I wanted to get a close-up," Good-to-Go says, as he returns to the shelter.

"You're crazy," somebody says.

"I thought you were going to get mauled," someone else adds. We're all shaking our heads, a bit disappointed that he got away with it.

After lunch Venado and I hike to Russell Field; it's one of the last shelters with a bear cage, a cyclone fence across the front of the shelter. Popeye tells us that people sometimes get in the bear cage and toss out food, trying to bait the bears in close enough to take pictures. "We're gonna try it tonight," he says.

At that I get up. "Come on Venado, we've got time to get to Spence Field." Venado grabs his pack quickly, and follows me down the trail—he's figured out that I have little interest in messing with bears. I explain that as the smallest hikers in our group, we, and more particularly, he, would be the bear's first choice to attack. We arrive at Spence Field in the evening, and find it crowded with college students and couple of older overweight guys, a profile that usually means snoring. Venado sets up our tent well away from the shelter, and I cook supper by flashlight.

Most hikers use headlamps, but we haven't made that technological leap; with the light clenched in my teeth, I spoon a gloppy pile of mac and cheese with tuna into Venado's bowl. I hang the light from a branch and we eat our suppers in heaping mouthfuls. "The weatherman says it's going to rain the day after tomorrow," I say, in between bites. "So we have to get out of here early if we want to get to Clingmans Dome and see the view."

Next morning we hit the trail at first light and eat breakfast on Rocky Top, a famous mountain straddling the North Carolina-Tennessee border. Pink and golden light grazes the ridge and diffuses across a misty valley. Venado tucks his hands into his vest to warm them. Another hiker passes and takes our picture up there.

The rocks have old dates carved into them, and names from back in the 1800s. "I think I saw a picture of Benton MacKaye up here some-where," I say to Venado. "It's one of those old nineteen-thirties black and whites of him and some other folks sitting up on a summit around here—near Rocky Top." I treat Venado to a chorus of the old tune—"Rocky Top you'll always be, home sweet home to me"—and clean up the breakfast dishes. "Come on, we have to go down through that gap and up again."

"How far is it?"

"Here's the book. Do the math."

We're ready to go, but Venado sits down with the book and calculates the miles, to the tenth. "Thirteen point three," he says. "And how far are we going today, altogether?"

"Not sure. Depends on if we can get water at Clingmans Dome. There's supposed to be water at the visitors center, but it's half a mile off the trail. Maybe we can go on to Mount Collins."

"How far is that?"

"Like twenty miles." I look at Venado to see how that sits with him. "Think we can do it?"

"Maybe."

It's a gorgeous day for hiking, cool and breezy.

"Poppy?"

"Yeah?"

"I have an idea for a sandwich."

"What?"

"A baguette with hot dogs and Hershey bars melted in it."

"That sounds truly delicious."

At Double Spring Shelter, I write in the register that we ate hot dog–Hershey bar baguettes that we got from a vending machine behind the shelter.

"I wonder if anyone will look behind the shelter for the vending machine," says Venado.

I laugh. "If they're thru-hikers they might get optimistic and take a peek."

Late in the day, close to seven o'clock, we hike along the high ridge towards Clingmans. The forest becomes familiar, full of fir trees, and it smells like home.

"How high is Clingmans Dome?"

"I already told you twice."

"But I get to ask three times."

I admit that I too forget, so we look in the book: 6,643 feet, and there it stands in the distance—close but far. As we come up to the summit another trail breaks off toward the visitors center, but we stick with the white blazes, heading for the top. A well-marked side trail spits us into a parking lot and we see a strange-looking tower with a wheelchair ramp spiraling up to a round observation platform. Late as it is, we run up the ramp, and quickly take in the view. We look at the plaques that show the names of the distant mountains.

"We're heading up there," I say, pointing to the highest ones. We take pictures of ourselves with blue sky and the far-off mountains as a backdrop, and then it's a race with the sun, and Mount Collins is another half mile off the trail. We make it, and cook supper in the crowded shelter. We meet Dos XX, who has slung his hammock under the spacious overhang.

"Are you the Barbarians?" he asks.

"Yeah."

"I've heard about you."

"Who are you?"

"Dos XX."

"Oh yeah, we've heard about you: the most interesting man on the trail." It seems like the first time we've seen him, but later he says he remembers me standing in the parking lot of NOC, reading from MacKaye's book to a bunch of folks.

Venado and I camp behind the shelter and it stinks of piss when the rain comes. In the morning we strike our wet tent and bundle our stuff under the overhang. Dos XX's hammock is gone. He left early, someone says, going to Gatlinburg to meet his girlfriend.

"I've been to Gatlinburg," I say. "In 1976, and I can't imagine it's improved. We're going to Cherokee."

After our twenty-mile day, Venado and I take an easy morning before heading to Cherokee.

Standing by the side of the road, hitchhiking in a light mist, we talk about our choice of resupply town. "The Cherokee were part of the Iroquois Nation, but they left and came down here," I tell Venado.

"Is it like a Native American village?"

"No, it's just a town on Cherokee land or something, and they have casinos."

We get a ride to town with an expert on the *Titanic,* and he joins us for a buffet lunch—all you can eat. There seem to be plenty of casinos and museums, but no one in town has alcohol for our stove. A young Cherokee woman named Angelwolf picks us up hitchhiking and drives us for miles in search of HEET.

We find it after more than an hour of prospecting and she drops us off back in Cherokee in the rain. A guy in a beat-up old car, a welder heading home to Tennessee, picks us up, and as we head back up into the mountains Venado spots elk.

"Poppy, look—there's the elk."

I look off to the side of the road and see two elk in a field.

"What are they doing?"

"They're reintroducing them," says the welder.

"Did they used to be around here?" I ask.

"Sure," says the welder. Venado nods, seeming to have known that.

The rain follows us to Icewater Spring Shelter, and lets up the next day as we hike to Tricorner Knob. Bluebell has sent us a spicy Indian dish for supper and we try it out, but it's so hot it makes us cry. Venado gives up and offers what he can't finish to another hiker, Hagar the Hungry. Hagar gobbles it up. He and his girlfriend, Poncho, who's taking a break from her job as a wilderness therapist to enjoy some wilderness for herself, are hoping to hike the entire trail.

A man in his sixties joins us late in the day, but he has no trail name. Venado calls him "White Beard," for very obvious reasons, and it sticks. Pretty soon we forget what his real name was.

Leaving Tricorner, I write in the log that we won twenty thousand dollars at the blackjack table in Cherokee, but lost it all again before we left. Some folks ask us later if it was true, and we smile.

The Smokies are good to us, something about high elevation—the views, the oxygen—that restores us. But all too soon we're descending out of the Fraser firs and back to the tulip poplars.

"I can tell we're going down," says Venado. "All the trees are changing."

"How do you feel about leaving the six-thousand-foot world?"

"Not good."

"It's nice up here isn't it?"

"Yeah."

"Down in the valley there'll be bugs and heat."

A few days later we come down out of the mountains into Hot Springs, North Carolina—the trail runs straight through town. Everyone shows up on cue: Popeye; Spoon; a couple of new guys, one of them six-foot-seven, named Giant, another with a southern accent, Louisiana Matt; Hagar; Poncho; and White Beard. We fill a couple of tables at the Smoky Mountain Diner and chow down on cheeseburgers, fries, and pie.

Popeye tells us about the bear cage. "It worked great," he says, "except the bears wouldn't go away and we couldn't get out for a while. It was all rain and fog when we got to Clingmans Dome; we couldn't see a thing."

We drink sweet tea, as the locals call iced tea, and wonder about visiting the hot springs that give the town its name. Too expensive, we all agree; better to go tubing in the French Broad River.

We're hiking on a credit card at this point; every expense is more debt and has to be considered, and avoided completely if possible. We're walking a fine line between being thru-hikers and being wood-land hoboes, and to save money, Venado and I camp outside town, on some flat ground across the river. Heading west, the French Broad flows into the Holston River and forms the Tennessee River, which, together with the Little Tennessee, flows into the Ohio, then the Mississippi, and finally the gulf.

"Can we go swimming, Poppy?"

"Sure."

Crossing the bridge back into town, we look down to see a group of teenagers tubing beneath us. A young woman in a bikini lies spread across a black inner tube, an American summer beauty.

"Papa, come on."

Under the bridge, we change into our shorts and wade into the water. Venado tries to coax me in deeper, but I resist.

"I don't like the smell of this river, Venado."

"It's fine."

"No it's not. Come on out of there."

"No Poppy, it's fine."

"No it's not; it smells bad and I'm not swimming in it." I back out and start getting dressed. Reluctantly Venado gets out of the water, though he continues giving me a hard time.

"Papa, it's fine."

"We have plenty of clean streams to swim in; we don't need to swim in this river."

We linger for an extra day in Hot Springs; in exchange for free beds and board we pick potato beetles off the potato plants in Elmer Hall's garden at the Sunnybank Inn—better known as Elmer's. At suppertime we find Elmer's table well laden, and we meet GoldenRay, one of several deaf and/or blind hikers attempting to thru-hike the AT, and we hit it right off, passing notes back and forth in a notebook GoldenRay keeps handy. Later that evening, I pick out a movie for Venado and me to watch on Elmer's DVD player, *Songcatcher*, based on the true story of Olive Dame Campbell, who collected songs from singers of the region—discovering many links to the oldest English folk music.

Elmer finds us watching the movie. "Did you know about this house when you chose that movie?"

We look at him, faces blank.

"This house belonged to Jane Hicks Gentry. She was the woman who gave them the songs."

"She was the songcatcher?" I ask.

"No, she was from here. She was the one who sang the songs for them."

"Huh," we nod.

"Isn't that funny?" I say. "I just picked it because I thought it would be appropriate for where we are, and it is."

"There's a sign out front that explains it. Did you read it?" Elmer asks.

"No. We'll check it out."

After reading the sign the following morning, we hike up out of the river valley on our first day of intense heat. Venado takes a drink from the bottle he filled at Elmer's. "This water tastes bad."

"It's the chlorine. I'm not too keen on town water. We should've filtered it."

Sweat pouring off us in the humid forest, we drink the town water in spite of the taste.

"This probably came right out of the French Broad," I speculate. "But it's all we've got."

A mile out, we cross a stream and dump our chlorinated town water in the dirt. As we filter good water from the stream, Spoon, Popeye, and Giant catch up with us and stop to change water too.

"There was a guy early on who said he thought the rise in giardiasis cases came from people drinking chlorinated water and it wipes all the good and bad microbes out of their systems," I say. "Then when they come out and drink wild water they have no resistance."

"I believe it," Spoon says. But like most hikers on the trail, he treats his water with a chemical solution—always.

"The way I see it, chemicals are the problem," I tell him. Having lived most of our lives on wild water and Mexican water, Venado and I use our judgment. When we find a spring, I often ask him, "What do you think? Filter or no filter?" And he gives an appraisal that I usually accept. When we can see the source are, and at high elevation and far from houses, and the water tastes good, we drink it straight out of the ground.

As the day wears on, we make our way along a rocky ridge heading toward Big Bald. Lightning flashes across distant gray clouds and thunder echoes round us.

"We better hurry along, Venado. We don't want to be up here if that comes this way."

Thunderstorms have been hitting us for the last week, soaking our shoes in five minutes and then leaving us to walk wet-footed for the rest of the day and the next.

"Papa, I can feel the water squishing in my toes," Venado says after slipping on his Tevas one such morning.

"Nothing like that feeling, is there?"

We get off the ridge and down into scrubby forest before the rain hits. Seeking refuge under a mulberry thicket, we hold our ponchos over our shoes, trying to keep our feet dry.

"You know what I notice since the river trip, Venado?"

"What?

"The way water flows, on the trail it's like little rivers, the way it eddies and breaks loose again, the same as the Nantahala."

"Yeah."

Our keep-dry plan doesn't work; the water floods us out, and for some reason I start singing the old Gordon Lightfoot song "The Wreck of the Edmond Fitzgerald." Dredging lyrics from my memory I teach it to Venado and it becomes our theme song. We hike on in a light drizzle, with our shoes wet, and the legend lives on from the Cheppewa on down . . .

At one point, Venado runs ahead and then off the trail to find a stick to whittle. But while he's in the woods whittling, I pass him by and take a fork down a hill.

Venado comes out and looks down the trail for me: nothing. He begins looking the other way: north. He blows several blasts on his whistle and heads north a short distance, down the hill. Seeing the mud torn with fresh footprints of someone sliding, he follows the tracks.

I hike along, thinking he got ahead of me, but not seeing any tracks, I begin to worry. When I reach a shelter and he is not there, I kind of panic. This is my worst nightmare. I head back along the trail, blasting away on my whistle, and finally see him coming toward me in tears, but I'm ready to harangue him anyway. Once we calm down, he explains what happened.

"The rain had just ended so I figured they must be your tracks, so I followed them," he says.

"Good thinking. Yeah, I slipped there. What about my whistle? Did you hear me blowing it?"

"No, did you hear mine?"

"No."

Two days later, we arrive at Erwin, Tennessee, on the Nolichucky River, another westward-flowing river that feeds into the French Broad a hundred or so miles downstream from Erwin. Unlike the French Broad—which flows through Asheville, North Carolina, a city of half a million people with a hefty manufacturing and agricultural base—the Nolichucky is relatively pristine.

On the way out of Erwin, Venado takes his long-sought swim. I lie on the beach near where a local family has set up camp.

"I heard that woman say 'oder' instead of 'older,'" I tell Venado after we leave.

Venado gets lost

"So?"

"It's kind of like hillbilly talk. It's interesting. Like the old songs in *Songcatcher*, the language here is very old, and it might be more like the way people spoke English hundreds of years ago. It's a kind of treasure."

We sleep near a whitewater rafting center, and grab showers there in the morning, plus a coffee for me. The heat increases and we climb to cooler country, Roan High Knob, the last of the six-thousand-footers until we get up north. Venado climbs ahead of me, one of those long fifteen-hundred-foot climbs with "our toes pointed up at the sky," as we've learned to say. And the summit seems to recede as we walk so that we can never arrive.

"This is one of those magic mountains, Poppy."

"Yeah, it doesn't want to let us climb it."

The thunder booms all around us, but the rain holds off as we race the storm up the mountain. I'm trying to focus on my breathing while Venado is talking away as usual. I tell him to let me know if he needs a rest. But he doesn't need one. We reach a flat spot and I ask him to stop—I need a drink of water.

"Poppy?"

"Yes?"

"Which travels faster, the thunder or the lightning?"

"We're homeschooling," I say, panting. "And you are in a great position to figure that out for yourself."

Venado looks over his shoulder at the towering dark clouds.

"The quiz'll be in five minutes," I tell him. But he tells me the answer a minute later. We reach the shelter at Roan High Knob just ahead of the rain, and after supper Venado is reading our guidebook.

"Poppy?"

"Yes?"

"It says we can go rafting on the Watauga River."

I shoot the idea down. The Watauga runs into the Holston and the French Broad Rivers. "It feels like these westward-flowing rivers are all sucking us backwards, and we need to move along. I want to get as far north as we can before your mom takes over. You two are only going to have about three weeks hiking together, and the closer we are to Harpers Ferry, the better chance you two stand of getting there in time to catch a ride north."

But days of rain drive us into two hostels in a row. Abby's Place, named for the owner's beloved deceased dog, is free, and the owner, Scott, trades us a pizza and sodas for a promise of getting one of my books mailed to him.

"I'm throwing in this Almond Joy for Venado," he says, handing us a frozen pizza, two Pepsis, and a candy bar. "There's an oven up there," he nods toward the bunkhouse. "Just follow the instructions on the package."

Up at the bunkhouse, Venado scores a new sleeping pad from the hiker box; it's lighter and softer than his army surplus Ensolite pad. We cook up the pizza, drink the cold, fizzy sodas, and split the Almond Joy.

"That guy Scott is okay."

"Yeah." Venado has his knife out, whittling.

"What are you making?"

"A cross for Abby. Scott said she's buried right here." Venado nods toward a stone marker in the garden.

Venado borrows my pen to write the dead dog's name on a flattened piece of wood, ties it to another, and pokes it into the ground. He tells Scott about it before we leave in the morning.

Scott thanks him, and we move on down the trail. In one of the registers we find an entry by Nature Boy, complaining about the depth of the snow, but that was some time ago and the trees and bushes now have their high-summer luster. Walking along, Venado plucks a large leaf from one bush and I can see from behind that he is busy doing something with it. He stops, turns around and holds a leaf mask up to his face. I can see the sparkle of his eyes through two little holes, and his smile through another, and I laugh. "Hold on, hold on, I gotta get a picture of this. You look like a little druid."

"What's a druid?"

"Oh no, here we go."

On another stretch of trail Venado walks ahead, working on a couple of rhododendron leaves. He stops and shows me how he has woven them together, trail art, and he leaves it on a stump. He asks people catching up to us if they noticed it, but no one has.

He often has something like that going, tying grass around his head so that it looks like antennae, or tying a leaf on a branch.

When we get to Kincora early in the day, after a short hike from Abby's, our old pal Cowboy offers to drive up from Boone, North Carolina, to spend the evening with us. He's off the trail, but he wants to see us, and he takes us into Hampton, Tennessee, a fading American town that's so quiet I ask Cowboy and Venado to sit down on the double yellow line of Main Street, and I take their picture with my iPhone. We eat sterile meals at a too-clean restaurant, and no one talks to us.

There's no Internet at the Kincora hostel, so I get into a lengthy discussion with three college guys from New Jersey who have come out for a section-hike at the start of their summer vacation. It turns into a sustainability seminar, with me explaining the principles of ecological economics. Venado sits on the floor listening.

"It's like in fisheries," I tell them. "Technological advances didn't help create more fish, they just enabled us to get what was left. It works like that in most natural resources." The young guys ask questions and I clarify my take on modern economics. "Depreciation of natural and social capital goes onto the accounts of companies and countries as 'profit.' The World Bank and everyone else knows this is going on— the artificial inflation of GDPs makes it easier for countries to borrow money." I look around to see if they understand. "Each generation is handed a world with fewer and fewer resources, ecosystem services and culture, and yet we're told it's worth the same as it was a hundred years ago. It's not. There is a major fraud going on and if I was you I'd be pissed as hell about it." They nod, and I can tell I've gotten somewhere with them, planted some seeds at least, even if they drift back to the dominant worldview.

"Do you understand what I'm talking about when I go on like that?" I ask Venado as we hike later in the day.

"Not everything, but I like hearing you talk about protecting natural capital."

I nod. And in two days we reach the eastern continental divide. A sign declares that all rivers flowing west go to the gulf, and those that flow east run down to the Atlantic.

"This is it, Venado. We're leaving the Tennessee River watershed. From here on out all rivers flow to the Atlantic"—or so I thought. We still had to cross the New River Valley.

Leave No Trace

The Leave No Trace philosophy of the wilderness recreation movement is kind of like recycling the planet: Leave the world as undisturbed as possible so that those who come behind you can enjoy an experience every bit as rich as yours. People use the same trails over and over, and everyone can draw a more-or-less equally valuable experience from an environment that remains pristine. There is a sense of caring that arises on the trail; we hikers form a community, and most of us go out of our way to protect the unspoiled quality of the wilderness we share with others.

Benton MacKaye saw watersheds as the geographical basis for community. He considered the forested mountains as vital to healthy watersheds, and a study he conducted in New Hampshire helped establish the White Mountain National Forest in an effort to safeguard New England's water supplies.

What MacKaye intended in creating the trail, replete with sustainable logging, agriculture, and industry, amounted to protecting watersheds. He saw those as the nation's productive capital, and believed economic activity should focus on collecting and equitably distributing the interest generated by natural resources. He understood, and based his views on, some very simple economic principles, one of which was that employment relies on access to resources, and one of the most critical resources on earth is water. He believed economies needed to emulate cyclical systems, like water flowing down to the sea, evaporating, and returning to the heights as rain.

By 1932 MacKaye described the United States' transportation system as a web of arteries without circulation, a one-way flow of the country's lifeblood from the wilderness and rural areas to the cities. MacKaye lamented that, unlike water, most resources took a dead-end trip through the economy and up the smokestacks or into the trash piles of civilization.

"Is there some rule of thumb for this vast consummation?" MacKaye asks in his 1951 essay "From Continent to Globe." "Verily," he answers himself, "the first and simplest rule on earth: give back to the earth that which we take from her. Return the goods we have borrowed; in short, pay our ecological bills. Pay them in dirt, not dollars."

This amounted to the concept of recycling. MacKaye proposed, among other things, that cities should compost their waste and ship it back to the farms, as some now do.

Biographer Larry Anderson reports that someone once said to MacKaye: "Damn it, Ben, nobody understands you because you're twenty years [or more] ahead of your time." The advocates of short-term interests maneuvered behind the closed doors of government and trumped MacKaye's recommendations over and over again, so that government policy seldom reflected MacKaye's forward-thinking philosophy. Writing again in 1951, MacKaye predicted that without balancing its ecological budget, humanity would "ultimately fail in preserving the earth as a habitable planet."

The trail was the one idea MacKaye had had that stuck.

Walking through thousands of acres of public lands, where at night the only lights Venado and I saw were stars and lightning bugs, we constantly had water on our minds. Always on the hunt for springs, we became vividly aware that those same springs are also sources of water for the cities in the Atlantic coastal plain that stretches from the Appalachians to the sea, and for the eastern half of the great Mississippi watershed. Yet because of short-sighted planning, most water flowing from the mountains ends up polluted, and every insult to it has to be redressed. The water must be treated, usually chlorinated, before people can drink it.

It seemed odd that so few people understood the full scope of MacKaye's idealistic vision for protecting the resources needed to generate economic activity. Finding it impossible to measure the monetary value of ecosystems and the cultures that understand them, our economic system calls them "worthless." But they obviously have value and should instead be considered priceless.

In Damascus, Virginia, Venado told some other hikers about an amazing huge orange and yellow mushroom along the trail. "Oh yeah, we saw that," they said.

Later, checking Facebook, I found at least two other hikers had taken pictures almost identical to the one I'd taken of that same mushroom. "I'll bet that mushroom has been recycled through the eyes of a thousand hikers," I told Venado. "Luckily no one 'harvested' it to make pharmaceuticals."

"Farm a what?" ∎

9

AN EYE
FOR DETAIL

Venado walks ahead of me almost all the time, often looking back over his shoulder to ask questions. I tell him not to turn around while walking or he's bound to trip.

"But Poppy, you fall down all the time."

"I don't recommend it."

We pass through a rocky area high on the side of a mountain, what I suspect is rattlesnake country, and I warn Venado.

"Poppy?"

"Yes?"

"What does a rattlesnake look like?"

"A rattlesnake."

"But when it's on the trail, does it look like a branch or something?"

I try to explain how to spot a snake, but miss the mark.

"But what does it LOOK like?" insists Venado.

I take a breath. "It doesn't look like anything," I finally realize. "It's invisible . . . until you see it. Then it looks like a rattlesnake."

And a few days later, Venado, walking twenty yards ahead of me, hears a startlingly loud buzz. You can hear the venom in that sound,

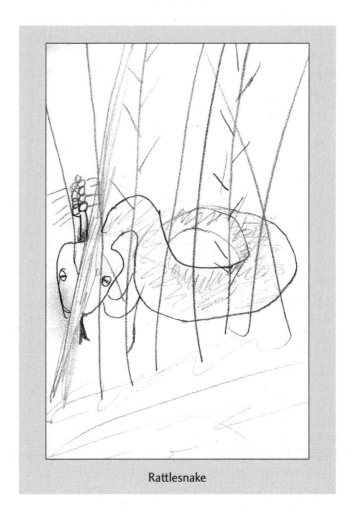

Rattlesnake

and it's coming from close to his leg. He jumps as far as I've ever seen him jump and then turns to look. There in the weeds beside the trail sits a fat rattlesnake, coiled to strike.

I come up and give it a wide berth. Finding a long stick, I use it to flip the snake away from the trail.

"Very lucky, Venado. I don't know what we'd have done if you got bit."

"Would I die?"

"Quite possibly."

119

Some of Venado's streams of questions flow from one day to the next. Goats, for example.

"Poppy?"

"Yeah?"

"Can a goat pull a cart?"

"Sure."

"What kind of goat is best for pulling a cart?"

"I don't know. That cashmere we had, what was his name?"

"Pickle."

"Yeah, Pickle. He would have been good for a cart."

"But he got aggressive."

"Yeah, it was a short trip to the sausage maker after he knocked you down."

The questions go on without interruption, day in and day out, as we wind along the trail, descending into hollows, crossing streams, and climbing back up to the ridge tops, to see what giants see.

"Are goats afraid of heights?"

"Baby goats?" I ask.

"No, all goats."

"Maybe some are. But they would have to get over it."

"Yeah, if a goat couldn't jump around on little ledges to get good grass, it would starve."

"Maybe they could get food delivered," I suggest.

"I don't think the Schwan's truck would go up into the mountains," Venado says, referring to a frozen food company in Maine.

"I guess not. No TV dinners in goat land."

On another day he's walking along like that, seemingly lost in a reverie about how to make a goat cart, and then:

"Poppy, stop!"

"What is it?"

Venado crouches down. "Look at this beetle. It's like a tank."

I stop and bend down to admire a stout brown beetle with a horn like a rhinoceros as it crawls across the ground like a little tank, pushing obstacles out of the way with its armored head. Fearless, Venado picks it up, but it pries itself loose and drops to the ground. "Did you see that, Poppy? He's so strong, he just pushed and *fooophh*."

One morning after a steep climb I step off the trail to take a rest on a flat rock with a survey marker on it. Venado drops his pack and takes a seat on a nearby rock. Reaching down between his feet he picks up a piece of chipped flint.

"Poppy, look. An arrowhead."

I take it and see the carefully formed notches for fastening it to a shaft.

"It sure is. Just the tip is broken off." I hand it back to Venado. "Good find. Where was it? Just sitting right there?"

"Yeah, I just looked down and saw it."

"I wonder how long that's been sitting there waiting for you."

"I can't wait to tell Mom."

"I am sure she will be thrilled."

Every mile we cover leads to something that requires investigation. When someone asks how many miles we do each day, I explain that we hike about fifteen miles a day, but that it takes *all* day. "We're the first out of camp in the morning and the last in, because we have to stop and look at everything—every peculiar rock, every bug. I'm not complaining, mind you. I get to see a lot of things I would otherwise miss."

Crossing the last of the balds, Hump Mountain on the North Carolina-Tennessee border, Venado dives into the grass and comes up with a two-inch-long beetle struggling to break loose from between his fingers.

"Watch it, he looks pretty ferocious."

"I don't know what it is."

"Me neither. I'll take a picture and maybe somebody on Facebook can tell us later."

Farther along, we encounter a herd of cattle, a rare breed with huge horns that someone had told us about. "They're called Watusi," I remind Venado. One has an odd pair of horns with one horn pointing up and the other pointing down.

"Can we go down there and take a closer look?"

"I'd rather not do any extra walking, especially down a hill I'll have to come up again."

"Can I go?"

I hand Venado my iPhone. "Here, take this and take a picture."

He runs down the hill toward the steers with the formidable horns while I start walking through the grass back to where we left our packs. Venado returns shortly and hands me the iPhone.

I look at the pictures.

"Hmmm. You didn't get very close."

"No."

Venado pulls open a ziplock bag full of trail mix and jams a handful of nuts, dried fruit, and chocolate chips into his mouth.

"How did Jeff Butt say these balds were formed?" I ask him as we sit on rocks, passing the bag back and forth.

"Giant sloths ate all the trees back in the ice age, and then people grazed their cattle up here, and now no trees can grow because all the roots are gone, and the giant sloths ate all the acorns so no oak trees can grow." He fumbles some trail mix into his mouth, smearing a bit of chocolate in the corners.

"What if you drop one of those pecans?"

Venado stops and looks at the ground, and then back at me.

Several hikers have pitched their tents and plan to camp up on the bald, enjoying the sunset and the cool weather. "I'm tempted to stay up here, Venado, but there's a hostel, Mountain Harbour, down in the valley that serves what they say is the best breakfast on the trail. What do you think?"

Venado is happy either way.

I call the number and learn that we must make a reservation the night before and get there by seven-thirty in the morning.

We debate it and decide to go for the breakfast, even if it means another hour of hiking. On the way down the mountain I call Mountain Harbour. "Book us," I tell the man on the other end of the line. "We'll be there at seven-thirty." Descending Hump Mountain in the last hours of light, we arrive at Apple House Shelter, a mile away from the hostel, and come upon our old friend Madstop. He started a few days ahead of us in Georgia, and when we first came upon his writing in the registers, we thought he was a twelve-year-old girl.

"I channel my inner twelve-year-old girl through the registers," he tells us.

"I can tell," I say. "It's those distinctive circles instead of dots over the i's."

Morning comes and we make our move before sunrise, aiming for the big breakfast. We arrive in the quiet of a still-sleeping hostel—a farm with outbuildings—and find our way to the bunkhouse. Up the dew-damp wooden stairs, we peek through the glass door and see a couple of guys sitting on a couch watching TV turned way down. I open the door and Venado follows me in.

"Are there showers in here?" I whisper.

One of the guys on the sofa points to a door off the main room.

In the bathroom, Venado showers while I do some quick laundry in the sink. I keep rinsing and rinsing and squeezing dark dirty water out of Venado's socks. Using hand soap, I scrub the shirts and shorts we've worn for three sweaty days and throw them into the shower for rinsing. Venado turns the shower over to me and takes a used towel from the hamper. In less than fifteen minutes we step out of the bathroom, showered, wearing our clean clothes, and carrying a plastic bag full of wet laundry.

Mountain Harbour turns out to be everything we had hoped for, and more. Piles of sausage, fresh fruit, omelets, bacon, toast, muffins, and pastries crowd the table; all you can eat for nine dollars each. We stuff our faces and buy a few extra snacks from the hostel store before heading back to the woods. The trail leads up through a steep meadow laced with other trails, and the white blazes come few and far between.

"Poppy!" Venado calls as I begin climbing past a tangle of paths. "Look, a white blaze." He points to where the trail turns out of the meadow and back into the woods.

"Good eye, Venado. Who would have thought the trail would not go up?" But soon after we slip into the trees the trail turns uphill again.

Rain pours down on us and hikers pile up at Mountaineer Falls Shelter. Dos XX shows up—he'd been visiting with his girlfriend again and had fallen behind us. White Beard, a couple of snorers from Georgia with their dog, and some new faces roll in as well. One—a gaunt vegetarian with round wire-rim glasses, a close-shaven head, and a little mustache—has no trail name.

"He looks like Gandhi," observes Venado, who saw Gandhi's image often when we lived in India. Everyone agrees, and soon no one can remember Gandhi's real name. The next morning, I find the snorers have left boots, insoles, dirty socks, and an assortment of food and gear

Black snake

all over the shelter table. I clear a place and cook breakfast. The sky promises more rain and Venado lobbies for a short day—he wants to play around the falls—and I concede to his wishes. Instead of bolting out ahead of the crowd, we lounge around all morning, bidding everyone farewell. It's a rare thing for us, but with wet laundry, we opt to build a fire and dry it out a bit.

Over the next week the weather clears out and the heat increases. Hiking along one day, Venado snaps his head to the left, looks at the ground, and leaps ahead. I look down; my eyes widen and I jump, tripping and stumbling in my rush forward. I scrabble over to where Venado stands and we both look back. Stretched out in the leaves next to the trail is the biggest black snake we have ever seen. Laughing off our nervousness, we look it over from a safe distance.

"It must be seven feet long," I marvel.

"Yeah, he's big." Venado adds, with admiring awe in his voice.

"I can't imagine hiking this trail without Venado's eyes," I say on a call to my wife. "He sees everything—racoon tracks, bugs. He spotted a little fledgling warbler sitting in a tree that I would have missed."

Despite seeing everything, Venado seldom seems to be focused on the trail, going on for days with questions about whether a buffalo is

Path picnic

stronger than an elk or a moose, kayaking, how boats sink, or things so wildly imaginative that I cannot fit them into my brain—how would we make snowshoes for elves? I do my best, explaining what I can, sometimes joining in the fun of making up impossibly ridiculous reasoning, but more often than not saying, "I don't know. We'll have to look that up."

Questions between us go only one way. When I ask Venado to solve some math problems, he puts no effort into it and gives wrong answers to questions he used to get right. Just north of Damascus, I throw a fit and threaten to end the hike. "What do you think we're out here for, Venado?!"

"To go to Katahdin."

"No! We're out here for education, and if you don't want to participate then you're just making a fool out of me!"

We chance upon a picnic two days later and a retired schoolteacher asks me about schooling on the trail. I tell her about the math incident. "Do you really chastise him for getting wrong answers?"

"Yes."

She tsks and shakes her head.

10

BACKFLOW: THE METROPOLITAN INVASION

"America is now in the midst of the fourth migration—the backflow. This is the push back from each central city into the suburbs and beyond. It is the invasion of the hinterlands by the metropolitan slum."

—Benton MacKaye

We take a three-day break in Damascus, our halfway point, and depart in the company of our deaf friend GoldenRay. In less than a week we pick up quite a bit of American Sign Language. One of the first words we learn is "water": a W formed with three middle fingers, with the index finger touching one's lower lip. Others we gather quickly are "thunder," "rain," "poop," "eat," "miles," "numbers"—all the critical vocabulary of hiking. Venado learns the entire sign alphabet and meticulously draws all twenty-six hand signs in one of the registers.

GoldenRay has the entertaining habit of liking to annoy annoying people. At one shelter where a father and his two sons have taken up the whole picnic table to organize their gear in the morning, Ray just shoves open a cooking space, knocking some of their food and sleeping pads to the ground. They yell at him and he smiles back. At another shelter, he sits up reading with his headlamp shining into the face of a guy who has been trying to order everyone else around all evening. The guy has his radio on after everyone has turned in, but he gets upset with GoldenRay. "Can you turn off your lamp?" he says to Ray. "It's shining right in my eyes."

"He's deaf," I tell the guy.

So the guy shouts as loud as he can: "Turn off your goddamn head-lamp!"

About a week into Virginia, mid-June, Venado, GoldenRay, and I cross Interstate 81, last seen, heard, and smelled in Pennsylvania. We follow a path under the highway—with trucks and traffic roaring above us—and break out into a muddy field. We cross a ditch littered with McDonald's bags, plastic bags, beer cans, soda cans, plastic oil bottles, and other uncategorized debris. A rainbow sheen of oil covers the water in the ditch, pretty to look at, but bad for everything else. GoldenRay looks at it and makes a face we don't need sign language to understand.

After a restaruant breakfast, we say goodbye to GoldenRay, who plans to hitchhike ahead and do some support work for other deaf hikers on the trail. On a less-busy highway we stop at a convenience store for some snacks and a bottle of HEET. Behind the counter a plump woman looks us over. "Are you boys hiking the trail?" she asks, and we tell her yes. "How far are you going?"

"All the way," says Venado.

"You're hiking all the way? How old are you?"

"Eight."

She fusses over him. "Come here and look at this." She leads us to a wall, covered with pictures of hikers on Mount Katahdin. "This one's my favorite," she says, pointing to a photo of a hiker.

"That's Nature Boy!" says Venado.

"We met him in Massachusetts, in April," I add.

"Yeah!" says Venado. "He was the first to get to Katahdin."

"Yes, he wrote to me. May twenty-eighth."

We yak away, and Venado tells her about the rattlesnake.

"How far can they jump?" I ask her.

"I've heard it said they can strike a third of their body length," she tells us.

"And what if they bite? What's the best thing to do?" I ask. "Do you cut the wound open and suck out the poison?"

"No they don't do that anymore," she tells us. "You can get gangrene and lose your leg. No, at most you put on a tourniquet, and let it off once in a while and try to get to a hospital as fast as you can."

"Do people die?"

"You can die, all right. It depends on the person, how big they are, and where they get bit."

Snake venom in the human body is like civilization in the wilderness; depending on variables like noxious fumes, noise volume, aesthetics, and scale, metropolitan inroads can poison a place to death. Once we've hiked beyond the vast federal forests of the TVA watershed, Venado and I begin seeing, hearing, and smelling a lot more of the metropolitan invasion. Not to say we mind completely; the trail through Pearisburg gives us a chance to eat fantastic Mexican food and watch a baseball game, but the cheap hotels, run-down main street, and strip malls make it look awful.

"Can we get a hotel, Poppy?"

"I'm not up for it. I don't want to be in a town."

But we cannot get away from it. The roar of superhighways reaches deep into the woods, and the trash left behind by too many weekenders robs the trail of its pristine feeling. All water sources have become suspect; the poison is everywhere. We camp outside town, in the glow and hum of the Celanese Acetate factory on the banks of the New River.

"Poppy, what are they making there?"

"I don't know," I say as we set up our tent. "But look, there's lots of bear poop around here. We better hang that food bag high high high."

While eating pretzel rods we scored in town, we pick apart the bear turds to see what they've been eating: lots of seeds, but no bits of hikers. The next day Venado finds a turtle shell, and later a live box turtle. We take a break while he draws a meticulous picture of its shell and waits patiently to see if it will peek out at us, but it never does, and I finally drag him away. "We need to leave the turtles alone," I tell him.

As we push deeper into Virginia, the roads grow more numerous, the water sources less frequent. At one point we approach an old farmhouse, hoping to fill our water bottles from a deep well. Cats bound around the feet of an old man standing in front of the house, and we ask if we can get water. The old man smiles and takes our water bottles into the house; the smell of cats wafts out the door when he opens it and Venado and I exchange concerned glances. But the man brings our bottles back, dripping and full of clear water.

Dry faucet

"I let it run awhile so it'd be good and cold," he says, and he tells us of a wonderful spring up by an old homestead. "We used to own it," he says. "We used to own all this land around here." We thank him and find our way back to the trail. Not far along, we come upon the old farm—abandoned wooden buildings green with moss and half collapsed—but the spring eludes us.

Many Appalachian hill people, like the family of the old man who gave us water, had found themselves caught in the middle between the metropolitan invasion and the preservationists. Instead of letting speculators buy up the land for development, the government buys it for preservation, and pays a meager price for it.

"Our family's farm in Pennsylvania would look like that one back there if it weren't made of stone," I say to Venado, as we hike on. "The state forced us out so they could build a dam, and then never built it. Fifty acres, a three-story stone barn, and a house built before the American Revolution—gone." Venado takes that in, and while I have made a commitment to not curse, it becomes sorely tempting.

"Your grandmother says if the state hadn't bought it, it would all be tract houses now. We wouldn't have been able to pay the taxes."

Venado has no old axes to grind; he lives in the present. At a stile over a barbed wire fence, he stops. Something has his attention; he squats down, reaches under a bush, and comes up with an unopened can of Mountain Dew, which we guzzle immediately.

Late in the afternoon, we cross paths with two other thru-hikers, Uncle Don and his nephew, TAAT (Total Animal on the Appalachian Trail). We'd met them earlier; Uncle Don, a lean man in his early sixties and dressed all in khaki, is hiking the AT to complete his triple crown—hiking the three major U.S. trails: the Pacific Crest Trail, which follows the Sierra Nevada up the west coast from Mexico to Canada; the Continental Divide Trail, which runs through the Rocky Mountains from New Mexico to Montana; and the Appalachian Trail. We've heard about the other trails, and Venado has asked if we can hike them when we've done the AT. "The PCT starts in the desert," I tell him. "When you can carry all your share of the food and a gallon of water, we'll talk about it. The CDT is the hardest, it's not even a marked trail in many places."

Venado greets our fellow hikers with news of our good fortune: "We found some trail magic—real trail magic—an unopened Mountain Dew."

Nonplussed, Uncle Don drops his pack, and mops sweat off his face. TAAT flops down on a log and holds his head in his hands. "Well, how much farther we got to go to the shelter?" asks Uncle Don.

"I have no idea," says TAAT.

"Couldn't be too far," I say.

"Well how far is it from that last shelter to this next one?" Don asks.

"Six point seven," says TAAT.

"What was the name of that last shelter?" I ask, and in spite of the fact that we had all stopped there, we struggle to recall, making a couple of wrong guesses. We're all woozy from the heat.

"Wait, wait, wait," says TAAT, "Laura's Creek?"

"That's it, that's it, Laurel Creek," I say. "We couldn't find the water there, and then we walked it by a little bit," I begin explaining, but mix up my words.

"No, we couldn't either," says Don, and TAAT voices assent.

"It said in the book to follow a blue blaze trail from the shelter," I say.

"And it said 'near the shelter,'" says Venado.

"Well our book says the other direction; it says it's south of the shelter. So I wrote in the register that it's north of the shelter."

"That's good," says Venado. "Other people might have that book."

An hour later we come to a cutoff where a weathered wooden sign reads "Sarver Hollow Shelter .3 miles" and points down a steep trail. TAAT and Don head down; Venado wants to stop there too, but I have to be firm. "We can't, Venado. Don't even think about it. If we stop here we will be short on food. We have to go to Niday if we want to get our mail drop tomorrow."

As it is, the mail drop is rather pathetic. We sort through a scant box with no lunches and powdered milk everywhere.

"The powdered milk opened up," says Venado.

"So I see. Bluebell must've been asleep when she put this beauty together."

At a store in Catawba, we buy submarine sandwiches, pepperoni, cheese, and a few other items before heading back to the woods and to Johns Spring Shelter, built by a man whose son died on the trail. The next day, we run into Don and TAAT again and agree to meet them for lunch at a restaurant just off the trail. "We're short on grub, so we might as well," I tell them.

The trail in southwest Virginia traverses several ridges that offer vistas of gentle farmland to the east and west. McAfee Knob juts out over a pastoral valley, and Venado stands out on the tip for me to take his picture. He's silhouetted against the morning sun, a tiny figure standing on that vulnerable finger of rock with all the mountains beyond him.

Water bottles left by boy scouts

From there, the trail leads back into the woods, and after running into a pair of bear cubs and navigating through a maze of megalithic rocks, we descend to a shelter. As I cut slices of pepperoni for our lunch, Venado turns to a sound, and we spot three hikers coming towards us, one of them a young boy.

"I think this is 4:17 and Scooter," I tell Venado. We have been in touch with the mother-and-son hiking team since early in our hike. Like us, they started in the middle and have come down to do the southern section before going back to finish the trail. They've chosen to hike this section from north to south—SOBO—and we have known for several days, via email, that they are heading towards us.

It's like a reunion of a family that has never met, and the boys take off to explore the rock maze while 4:17 and her hiking pal, Etch-a-Sketch, and I lounge at the shelter, comparing notes and stories. The boys return with reports of discovering a turkey nest in the rocks. "We left it alone," they say.

Like us, Scooter and 4:17 have to make the miles, and after an all-too-brief visit, we head our separate ways, continuing along the ridges of Virginia. At another rock outcrop, Venado goes exploring, climbing down in the cracks.

"Papa!" he calls, excited.

"What?" I jump up from making lunch and run to the crevasse his high-pitched voice is coming from.

"Papa, there's a box down here with all kinds of things in it."

"Leave it alone."

"But it has all these things in it!"

He holds the box out where I can see it. It's a little Tupperware container filled with all sorts of odd things. "Better bring that up here and we'll have a looky."

He brings it up and we start to pick it apart. Inside we find a granola bar, which we immediately eat, a pencil, a lighter, a little carabiner, and a note.

"What's it say?"

Venado reads it, and hands it to me.

"Geocache. I guess people go hunting for these boxes with GPS things. I think we're supposed to take something and then put something in."

"We took the granola bar," Venado reminds me.

"So what do you want to put in?"

Venado takes a bandana he found and puts it in the box. I grab a couple of promotional bookmarks out of my pack and contribute them to the geocache.

"Good work, Venado. Now go put it back where you found it and we'll get outta here."

As the summer heat intensifies, we hike early and late, filter water from creeks in the valleys, and camp up high where the breeze blows cool and the mosquitoes are scarce. After Don and TAAT pass us for the last time south of Daleville, Virginia, we come out of the woods onto a big highway. We stand there a minute, surrounded by superstores, chain restaurants, and cars and trucks racing by—it's the outer edge of the Roanoke metropolis. Although we practice "leave no trace" in the woods, this is our trace, the industrial world that supports our hike in many ways, including an outdoors store in a shopping mall a half mile west of the trail. We have both worn holes right through the soles of our shoes.

"Can we get new shoes there, Papa?"

"We'll get some for you. I'll be off the trail in a few days."

In town, we get Venado some new footwear, and, hanging out at a restaurant afterwards, we get into such an animated conversation with the folks behind the counter that we leave without paying.

Back near the trailhead, I reach into my pocket and pull out a twenty-dollar bill. "I had this when I went to town," I tell Venado. "We forgot to pay for our lunch." But we don't go back; we head up the trail with Venado sporting a pair of new Keen sandals, bright blue with yellow patches on the soles.

Between Daleville and Troutdale we flush a little fawn out of the tall grass. "We could have caught it with our hands," says Venado, delighted. And after crossing route 81 again and hiking three miles into the woods, we come around a bend in the trail and plow into the back end of a big bear.

When Venado and I meet a bear—and we meet them regularly—the question always arises: How will this work out? But in spite of the horror stories we hear, our bears always run away in a hurry, and this one is no exception.

The massive black bear looks over its shoulder, sniffs, and then dives down the hill. "Poppy, I thought you said bears couldn't run fast downhill."

"That's what I was told, but I guess I was wrong. He seemed to move right along." Venado wants to camp here, where the bear lives.

"If we camp here we'll have to hike twenty-three miles tomorrow. You up for that?"

"Sure."

I have not been extremely enthusiastic about Venado's mother coming out to hike. While I had professed that the hike was all about him, I do have some attachment to doing the whole thing together; but I have to let go of that, and the fact is, I need a rest.

"Why is she coming out?" people ask.

"Well she is paying for it, and she wants to enjoy some of the fun," I say. "Besides, my feet are killing me and so is this heat. I'm glad for a break."

When I ask Venado how he feels about his mom taking over, he shrugs. "I'm fine with it either way. I like hiking with you, but it will be fun to hike with mom, too."

The following day, we cross the Blue Ridge Parkway six times and never get out of earshot of the scenic highway. At dusk on the eve of the Fourth of July, we descend into Jennings Creek to the sound of an outdoor rock concert. By the time we make camp, we can hear fireworks, but Venado is asleep, and after slogging more than twenty-three miles on perpetually sore feet, I do not get out of my sleeping bag to look.

11

SEAWEED

Next morning, Venado and I walk a mile down the road to a camp-ground and, having become proficient hoboes, cadge showers again. In the camp store/restaurant we buy cheeseburgers and french fries for breakfast. The night before, we had found a bottle of Dr. Pepper with the seal broken on the cap. It was almost full, and tempting. When I'd twisted the cap—*pffft*—it had fizz. I'd taken a sip and Venado wanted some too. "No, Venado, we don't know who drank from this or what kind of diseases they may have," I'd told him.

"But you drank some," he had argued.

"Just a little." Our desire for that fizz and sugar had overwhelmed our prudence and my weak argument, and we'd polished the bottle off. Amazing what happens to your sensibility after months of deprivation.

"What time is mom getting here?"

"If she left from Philly at five this morning, I can't see her getting here any sooner than one or two o'clock this afternoon, maybe later."

After a long breakfast and doing laundry, Venado and I head back to our camp. It's nearly noon and the sun has come into the valley full force, bringing southern-style heat and humidity with it.

"We need to find a nice swim hole."

"Yeah."

Walking along the narrow road through the lowland woods full of vines and young trees, we follow the edge of a creek that has a tinge of the French Broad odor to it. A small black car approaches, heading right for us and slowing down. The trees overhead reflect in the windshield and we cannot make out the driver. I push Venado off to the side.

"What?"

"Watch it—I don't know what this nut is up to."

The car stops, the driver's side door opens, and out pops Venado's mom, smiling her big toothy smile. "Hey there, hikers!"

Venado runs to her and gets a big hug, and so do I.

After a lengthy greeting, we pile into the new car and drive to the pavilion that marks the free camping area. Another family has taken it over for their picnic so we shift to a more secluded spot further down the creek. Venado tells his mom about the Dr. Pepper the night before.

"Blechh," she says.

He tells her about our cheeseburger breakfast and shows her his new shoes as we spread our gear out across two picnic tables, and prepare mom for the trail. She has brought a new Deuter backpack—two pounds lighter than mine—and on my recommendation she has hiking poles and a knee brace. "I've seen a lot of tall people like you with knee trouble," I'd emailed her. "I think you would benefit from hiking poles, and a brace if you need it—no pun intended."

We sort out the food she's brought, including a big packet of dulse—a dried Maine seaweed that Venado has been missing—and healthy snacks. Venado and I go over our systems with her. We sort out the mainstays of the menu—muesli and powdered milk for breakfast; cheese and pepperoni on tortillas for lunch; mac and cheese with tuna, or chicken and rice, for supper; dried fruit, energy bars, and gorp for snacks. I explain how we soak our rice in a water bottle all day so it will cook up quickly in the evening. I tell her how much fuel we carry, eight to sixteen ounces, and who carries what—I have most of the meals; Venado takes snacks, extra water, and whatever else we can jam into his little pack. We do trail maintenance in whatever ways we can, we tell her—mostly picking up trash and clearing manageable branches off the trail. We both carry trash bags, and usually stuff our pockets full of energy bar wrappers and microtrash we pick up along the trail. We describe what we wear in the rain (ponchos and leggings), how much spare clothing we carry (very little), and how we use garbage bags for pack covers. I go over the list of little essentials like the trail guide, the BIC lighter, spoons, and the windscreen for the stove, and by the time we have everything sorted the day has grown oppressively hot.

A small stream feeds into the creek, and on a secluded stretch we take turns wallowing in a deep hole until everyone gets cooled down. I look at my beautiful wife drying off in the sun: her long, wavy, dark hair, her thin, muscular body, her knobby knees and long toes.

She has brought an extra tent for this one night we have together, and Venado takes it hard when we tell him he will be sleeping alone in his tent. "Just this one night," I say. "You've had me for months and you'll have mom for weeks."

It's hard to say what the trail has done for my wife and me, but all talk of a breakup is off the table.

"You've changed," she says when we're alone.

"You too." We smile. "I think the endless walking out here, it strips me naked emotionally. I realize I love my children and the best thing I can do is figure out how to stay with you, which is not too bad."

She wrestles me. "Think you can stand it, do ya?"

"That woman who left us on the road in Vermont? I can love her a long time."

"Why?"

"I think because you were taking care of yourself and not blaming me, or expressing some disappointment with me. That's what I'm done with: exchanging disappointments."

"I'm starting to believe you."

It's mushy, but having survived the kind of storm that has torn so many of our friends' families apart, we indulge ourselves.

It's hard to say what has shifted for us. I've become fond of saying that on the AT, all the ego stuff gets worn away in the simple struggles to stay fed and dry, to find water and a comfortable place to sleep. "Out here, life has meaning for me," I tell my wife. "For the first time since becoming a father, I can do it the way I want. I can teach my children the things that I think are important in a place that is real. I'm not just fulfilling expectations."

Before starting the trail, I had gotten it into my head that life had become a boring suburban trap; even though we lived in the country, the value system was homogenous and suburban, and I wanted out. I had felt I wasn't getting any love or respect. I had felt we had all fallen into what I called "disappointment addiction," where we constantly expressed our disappointment with each other and ended up walking on eggshells and apologizing all the time.

"I'm not doing that anymore," I'd said. "I'm not going to criticize anyone anymore." And to everyone's surprise, I've stuck to my word, more or less—old habits are hard to break.

Somewhere in the process of hiking the last twelve hundred miles, our attitudes have changed. The Vermont incident was important, but I feel we are all awakening in a much bigger way. MacKaye believed in the primeval world's metaphysical power to heal people emotionally, physically, and spiritually, and perhaps the best explanation for the positive shift in our feelings is: AT alchemy.

In the morning, a car key is placed in my hand. "When was the last time you drove a car?"

"Last September."

"Please be careful."

I carry my beloved's pack up the first hill, and we search for a trail name for her. She comes up with one, but it's not sticky. We try to saddle her with her household nickname, "The Health Minister," but she refuses, and heads into the woods nameless. Guided by her little boy, Venado, skipping down the trail ahead of her, she walks away, and like deer or bears, the two of them vanish among the trees.

Back on the road I get behind the wheel of a brand-new car and roll effortlessly along the asphalt trail to the I-81 on-ramp. It all comes back to me. The tractor trailers, the roadside restaurants, the big green signs telling how many miles to somewhere. After a few stops to interview the leaders of some projects I suspect Benton MacKaye would have liked, I head north again, covering in a matter of hours the distance it has taken us months to walk.

Late in the evening, I stop at Waffle House and order a full breakfast. Discreetly, I take out my iPhone, turn on the video camera, and slowly pan it around the brightly lit restaurant, capturing the chatter of well-fed people sitting in front of plates full of waffles and such. Near midnight, I arrive at my parents' house outside Philadelphia to pick up my daughter, who has stayed with them for the last two weeks. Intent on doing some home renovation in the three weeks my wife will be on the trail, we leave early the next morning and drive straight through to Maine.

A few days later, I get an email: The other thru-hikers have christened my wife "Seaweed" because of the dulse she carries in her food bag. She loves the trail, and she has lost her cell phone. I FedEx her a spare phone and put together a food box for Waynesboro, Virginia.

Seaweed finds that, as predicted, Venado has an ample supply of questions. And when he runs out of new ones, he hits her with old ones, or maybe he is looking for consensus.

"Who would win in a fight between a buffalo and a moose?"

"The moose, I would think," replies Seaweed.

"No, a buffalo; Papa found a YouTube of a fight between a buffalo and an elk and the buffalo won."

"Venado, did you already ask Papa these questions?"

Seaweed doesn't get much of a response. "Maybe," says Venado.

Seaweed writes to me: "Venado may aim to be an AT thru-hiker, but he's still an eight-year-old child testing out his worldview with an overwhelmingly creative array of hypothetical ideas. Walking the trail happens to be what he is doing while the more significant growth is manifesting between the ears, as they say."

Venado's questions continue: "What about between a saber-toothed cat and a . . .?" Seaweed begins to answer as Venado dives into the brush.

"Look at this cool beetle."

"Oh my god, he's huge!" says Seaweed, leaning close to look at the two-and-a-half-inch-long black beetle with long legs scrabbling wildly to get out of Venado's persistent grip. "Amazing."

They send reports up to Maine, about their new hiking family: eighty-year-old Zeus, Huff-n-Puff—who gives Venado a first-rate compass—and Princess Doa, a skinny woman who hikes faster than they do but waits for them, so that they share shelters with her more often than anyone else.

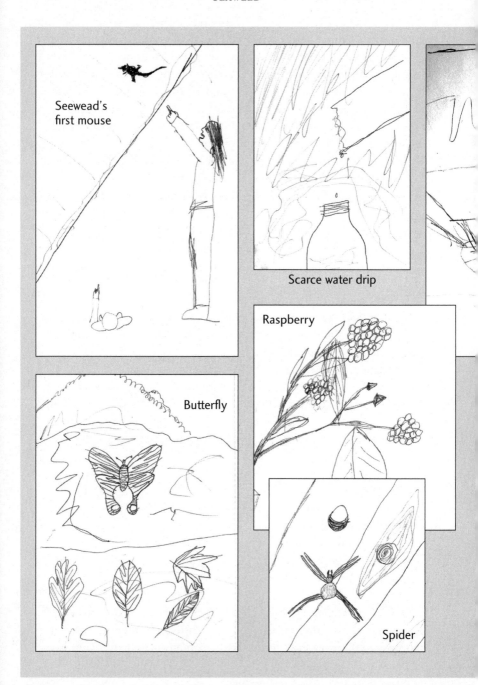

Seewead's first mouse

Scarce water drip

Raspberry

Butterfly

Spider

Chasing a deer out of camp

Young deer

Venado finds a knife

Venado and Seaweed do not have the iPhone, and the Barbarian Utopia Facebook page grows quiet. With their communication reduced to a minimum, Venado's pictures tell their story.

After Seaweed and Venado have been on the trail a week, the phone in Maine rings. It's Bob Stuart, a reporter from Waynesboro; he wants to do a story on the eight-year-old AT hiker and his mom.

"Stuart? Any relation to James Ewell Brown Stuart?" I ask, using the full name of the famed Confederate cavalry general J.E.B. Stuart.

"Yessir, I'm proud to say he was my great-great-grandfather."

"Well, my great-great-grandfather fought on the Union side at Chancellorsville, and took some wounds at Gettysburg. No hard feelings, mind you," I say.

"None at all."

But a Civil War discussion between a native Pennsylvanian and a Virginian is not the point of the call. Bob's concern is the press of civilization on the trail. "They're trying to put new housing developments right up against the trail and I'm doing a series of stories on how important the trail is. Do you think I could meet with your wife and son? I think they'd make a good story."

I help Bob set up a meeting with Venado and Seaweed at the YMCA campground in Waynesboro at the end of the week, and the article runs online shortly thereafter.

Stuart writes a simple piece that outlines the hike and all its benefits. He highlights Venado's eagerness to continue to Katahdin, quoting Venado as saying: "Yeah, I'm tired, but I'm not tired of doing this."

Stuart's less-than-objective article is part of a series he is writing, lamenting the impact of development along the trail corridor, and he frames a quote from Seaweed from that point of view: "She said the Appalachian Trail is 'beautiful and a blessing in this day and age' when one considers development in the U.S. 'I hope it will remain wild and free.'"

From what I have seen, the trail comes under attack from the inside too. The trail as it now exists does not offer the nature centers or the camps and the skill-building work of logging and farming. It often becomes a playground for predominantly white urbanites and suburbanites who realize they want to connect with the primeval environment but haven't always learned how to do it with respect. Shelters are trashed with garbage and graffiti. People toss uneaten food into the woods, or wash their dishes in the streams. We all fail to follow the proper trail etiquette at times; I seldom dig my cat holes very deep, for instance—though that karma will come back to haunt me later.

The innocence and sensitivity that Venado has brought to the woods stand in stark contrast to the party animals he occasionally crosses paths with. For his part, Venado never sees them as anything other than fellow hikers. He notices that they curse a lot, and that their jokes often go over his head, but he doesn't judge them. He laughs with them, and when chance permits, he brings them to his level with stories about the deer and bears and bugs and turtles that he never fails to notice, things they may have missed.

Benton MacKaye once said he did not understand thru-hiking, or speed hiking on the trail. "I would give a prize to the person who hiked it the slowest," he told *Backpacker* magazine in 1972. He would have smiled on Venado and his mother, who on one scorching day, hike a meager five miles.

An AT ridge-runner takes some photos of Seaweed and Venado crossing the James River footbridge, and she emails them to me as they near the end of their hike. Seaweed, in her pigtails and yellow Capri pants, stands smiling next to a contemplative-looking Venado. In a shot of them walking across the bridge you can see the bounce in Venado's step, the bright blue Keen sandals splashing color next to the same dirty shorts and T-shirt he has worn for three months.

Seaweed has a friend heading north from Maryland to Vermont on July 30, but at the rate she and Venado travel, we wonder if they will reach Harpers Ferry in time to catch a ride. In a final surge, they pull it off.

"We night hiked!" Venado tells me over the phone.

"Night stumbled," adds Seaweed in the background.

The Modern Barbarians

*"And who are these modern Barbarians? Why we are . . . as the Civilizees
are working outward from the urban centers we Barbarians must be
working downward from the mountain tops."*

—Benton MacKaye, 1927

As mentioned earlier, MacKaye intended the Appalachian Trail to be
more than a hiking path; he saw it as a place where people could
"breathe oxygen," as he liked to say, and restore their mental and physical
health in the outdoors. The communally owned camps he hoped to
establish would be modeled after Camp Tamiment, which operated in the
Pocono Mountains of Pennsylvania between 1921 and 1963. All the bunga-
lows at Camp Tamiment had been built with wood cut from the camp's two
thousand acres and milled at the camp's own sawmill. MacKaye wanted to
incorporate nearby farmland into the camps so that crops could be grown
for sale and to supply the camps' kitchens. He hoped these camps would
become teaching centers for forestry and sustainable livelihoods. In 1921 he
wrote:

> Food and farm camps could be established as special communities
> in adjoining valleys. Or they might be combined with the community
> camps with the inclusion of surrounding farm lands. Their develop-
> ment could provide tangible opportunity for working out by actual
> experiment a fundamental matter in the problem of living. It would
> provide one definite avenue of experiment in getting "back to the
> land." It would provide an opportunity for those anxious to settle
> down in the country: it would open up a possible source for new,
> and needed, employment. The trail, in effect, would be a sluiceway,
> channeling people's desire to reconnect with the land into a pro-
> ductive learning experience.

It seems plausible that some people might still be willing to follow that path, and informal manifestations of MacKaye's idealistic vision have materialized all along the trail, from us working for room and board in Elmer's garden in Hot Springs, North Carolina, to Moon in the Pond Farm, where Dom understood and embraced MacKaye's idea of a farm camp.

Before leaving the South, I went off the trail to connect with people I'd heard about who were doing things I felt MacKaye would have been proud of. First stop was Wilderness Adventure at Eagle Landing and a meeting with director Gene Nervo, "the Colonel."

Venado and I had met one of their groups at the Audie Murphy Monument, a quiet spot in the woods of Virginia, north of Pearisburg, not far from where the World War II hero died in a plane crash in 1971.

"You should come visit the school," the instructors told us. "There is a big open house on the Fourth of July." We didn't make it.

But on July 5, I cruised through rural Virginia and arrived at the Wilderness Adventure campus, an array of stylish wooden buildings spread over four or five manicured acres. Before lunch, Gene's son showed me around the control center of the wilderness school: Computers and radios crowded the many desks; the walls were covered with whiteboards filled with lists of names and locations of students, along with lists of upcoming courses. After the tour, I met up with Gene.

"It's a shame you weren't able to make it out here yesterday," Gene told me. "We had a barbecue."

"I'm sorry. I had no vehicle."

Gene took me to the dining hall and invited me to dig in to their everyday smorgasbord. No problem.

The fact was, Gene confided, the wilderness courses that used to be the backbone of the school had taken a backseat to leasing the campus out for conferences and weddings. "At first I thought it was just us," Gene said. "But everyone's down. Outward Bound, NOLS [the National Outdoor Leadership School] are all cutting courses."

"What do you think's going on?" I asked.

Gene looked me in the eye with an expression of concern mixed with sadness. "My guess is they're sitting in front of computers," he said. "Kids aren't interested in the wilderness. Their parents are afraid."

Gene's courses rarely use the trail. The ATC does not encourage "for-profit" companies, such as Wilderness Adventure, putting wear and tear on the public trail and filling up the shelters. But the school's objective of getting folks out into the wild remains as a vestige of MacKaye's ideal. At Wilderness Adventure, city kids can rediscover a deeper capacity for awareness in the wild, where sounds, sights, and smells do not numb the brain. Stimulation becomes subtle enough that their bodies regain some of their primal sensitivity, as when Venado and I had stepped out onto the highway in Pennsylvania and the stink of it surprised us. Apparently, it didn't bother us when we lived in the thick of it, because we were desensitized; enough time in the woods and we became resensitized.

Gene understood the value of awakening that awareness in kids. His own connection with the wild began in New York City, of all places. "Washington Heights Park was only a block from my house," he told me. "My friends and I spent all our time there. There were these cliffs that went down to the East River—we used to find bats and all sorts of things there. After we moved to New Jersey I got involved in scouting, not that I was much of a scout—I just liked to go camping, and we went at least once a month, year round."

MacKaye preached the benefits of rural experience as well, and Gene got that on his grandmother's farm in Liberty, New York. "My brother and sister and I would spend all summer up there. They milked their cows by hand and my uncle did all his work with horses. That was in the late forties, early fifties. I've been around a while," he said with a laugh.

Gene spent over thirty years in the marines, and since 1990 he had been sending kids as young as eight—Venado's age—out for short trips and doing wilderness skills and ropes courses at the Virginia campus. "It's important in so many ways," Gene said. "Mostly it's about confidence building and creating a relationship with nature. Kids who form that relationship early generally maintain it for life. And they will protect nature." The passion in his voice and manner made it clear that Gene's soul was in his mission. He and I hit it off great—as we spoke, we found ourselves following the same trains of thought—and he wished me the best of luck with my project, sending me down the road with a sandwich for later. Gene's views hearkened back to something our friend Jeff had said when Venado and I hiked with him in Pennsylvania.

"What worries me is that the kids who grow up disconnected from nature will someday be sitting in our state legislature, and they won't understand the value of all this," Jeff had said, sweeping his arm around in the woods. "They'll be fine with selling state lands for development." It was an ominous thought, and already a problem in many places we passed.

On the way to Roanoke, I stopped at the restaurant where Venado and I had eaten three days earlier. "I was in here with my son the other day," I told a bemused young guy behind the counter. "I had a salad and my son had nachos and a milkshake, and we all got talking and I think we left without paying."

The guy behind the counter shrugged. "I don't think anybody noticed."

"But I'd like to pay. I don't want thru-hikers to get a bad name."

"Really, don't worry about it," he said. "It's on us."

So I didn't worry, and drove on across Roanoake.

"Farm camps might ultimately be supplemented by permanent forest camps through the acquisition (or lease) of wood and timber tracts. These of course should be handled under a system of forestry so as to have a continuously growing crop of material. The object sought might be accomplished through long term timber sale contracts with the Federal Government on some of the Appalachian National Forests. Here would be another opportunity for permanent, steady, healthy employment in the open."
—Benton MacKaye, "An Appalachian Trail," 1921

Following another set of complex directions into the countryside, I made my way to the farm of Jason Rutledge, a champion of sustainable logging. Jason operated a logging business and nonprofit organization, the Healing Harvest Forest Foundation. His mission—to address human needs for forest products while creating a nurturing coexistence between the forest and the human community—sounded like something right out of MacKaye's playbook.

Jason did not believe in clear-cutting or high-grading—cutting only the high-value trees and leaving everything else. He preferred holistic logging. "Logging for the future," as he called it. "If conventional forestry, particularly when practicing 'liquidation' even-aged management or clear-cutting, is seen as 'fast-food logging,' then our practices are home cooking with natural ingredients," said Jason. And while he did use a chainsaw for cutting, he used horses to get the wood out, and he harvested selectively and carefully with an eye towards regeneration as opposed to profit maximization. "When the forest is seen as a 'natural capital system,' or a financial institution such as a bank, then if you own the bank, it would be best not to rob it," said Jason.

MacKaye believed in technology and progress; it's unclear whether he would have supported horse-powered logging over the use of skidders and other machinery in the woods. Certainly, the noise and smell of the diesel-powered machines would not have been a plus for the wilderness experience. Perhaps the residents of his imagined camps would have used all hand tools and horses in order to protect the blessed quiet of the woods.

When I arrived at Jason's farm, it appeared the horseman had left suddenly. Two muscular Belgian draft horses stood out in a hard-grazed field with a pile of hay at one end. A hose filling a trough for the horses had been left running and the water spilled over the trough's edge, making a growing puddle in the field. I found the valve and shut it off. I hollered . . . no answer. I walked down to a house that looked out on the field—nobody home.

I walked around the field to a beautiful barn and gave myself the tour while waiting for Jason to show up. A dog lying on the floor of the barn barely gave me a second look. A two-wheeled horse cart hung suspended by block and tackle from the ceiling. Horse collars and harnesses hung from the walls in empty stalls; tools and welding equipment filled a work room; guitars, drums, and a sound system in another room indicated Jason's penchant for making music. I was content knocking around his farm, waiting. I took photos, killing time. I tried to interview the horses, but they refused to answer any questions. I pulled fresh green grass for them and fed it to them over the fence. After an hour I got back in the black Honda and headed down the road, loading up on fresh cherries and peaches at a farm stand along the way.

"There was an emergency," Jason told me later, over the phone. In a lengthy conversation, I finally asked how he found his way to forests as a way of life. "Was there some defining experience in your youth that brought you here?" I asked.

"There sure was," he said. "I was raised by my grandfather and grandmother. My mother was fifteen years old when I was born—that was in nineteen-fifty—so my grandparents raised me. My grandfather was an illiterate sharecropper. He did all his farming with horses and mules. He was proud of his work, and he found his own sense of dignity in that," Jason said with pride. "I grew up in the shadow of that man, and I think I captured some of that without knowing it. I call it the human dignity dividend that comes from doing good work that you love and believe in." When Jason got out of the service in 1968, he found his way back to the simple way of life his grandparents had modeled for him. "I found that going back to the countryside was good for my mental health."

"I know what you mean," I told him.

When I had set up our Facebook page, "The Barbarian Utopia," I had hoped it would go viral and draw us some much-needed sponsorship. When I had to choose a category for it I had chosen "Education." As far as personal pages go, it had proven very successful, but it missed the mark of thousands of "likes."

"Do you think it's the name?" My wife asked at one point. I shrugged. I hadn't thought about it. I just liked the sound and the idea as expressed by MacKaye. But her question had forced me to reconsider the way I threw the word *barbarian* around and embraced it.

At home, I spent a week trying to answer the question. The word comes from the Greek *barbaros*, meaning foreign, and modern English dictionaries define it as meaning rough, uncultured, brutish, and so on.

But history sheds a different light on the barbarians, and that was where MacKaye drew his reference. For a thousand years, various barbarian tribes had come from the wilds of Europe and Asia and integrated themselves into Roman civilization. They had filled in the gaps and picked up the slack in places where the empire failed.

As the Roman Empire had crumbled, those gaps got wider, and eventually the barbarians had taken control of what remained of a civilization that had worn itself out through excessive wars, declining agricultural production, and cultural narcissism. In the end the barbarians had become the guardians of Western civilization.

Like MacKaye, Gregory of Tours, a sixth-century historian, had seen Frankish barbarians as having "passed over the decadent Gallo-Romans like a purging fire."

12

VOLUNTEERS

"Two weeks spent in the real open—right now, this year and next—would be a little real living for thousands of people which they would be sure of getting before they died."

—Benton MacKaye, "An Appalachian Trail," 1921

Truth be told, I think there is a little Barbarian in most people, a deep-seated need to cast off the stultifying obligations of civilized life, if only for a moment. As Seaweed and Venado finish up their southern hike, we make a date for the whole family to meet back in Vermont, and after a grand reunion at Breeze and Robin's in Brattleboro, Seaweed leaves Venado, Blue-ish (formerly Bluebell), and me on the Stratton-Arlington Road on August 1.

"Why did you change your name?" Venado asks his sister.

"Because I wanted something different, and I say 'ish' all the time."

Again, we sort out our gear at the exact spot where we got off the snowy trail back on May 1. Things have changed—the trailhead parking lot abounds with cars sporting license plates from all over New England. Peak season has arrived.

On top of the venerable Stratton Mountain, where many believe Benton MacKaye first envisioned a trail running the length of the Appalachians, we meet a crowd of Hasidic Jews on holiday from New York. We've been on the trail a few hours, and I break out the lunch fixings as Hasidim boys with yarmulkes and earlocks dangling and girls and mothers in long dresses all crowd round, full of questions for us. Blue-ish, reluctant to engage, refers all questions to me. Venado disappears into the woods, exploring.

What do you eat? How do you get food? they ask. Where do you sleep?

I explain our food supply system, the boxes of noodles, muesli, tuna, cheese, pepperoni . . . But every answer leads to more questions. Distracted in putting together the lunch tortillas, I drop a slice of pepperoni on the ground. With hardly a thought I pick it up, brush the dirt off, and slip it into a tortilla. When I look up, I can see the concern on one mother's face.

What about school? asks another.

Venado bursts out of the woods with his hands full of moldy bones. "Look, moose bones!"

The Hasidic kids stare in wonder at the bones. Venado tries to hand them some.

A little girl reaches out. "Don't touch that," a mother's voice calls in a hushed way. As Venado continues to offer, a woman's protective arm reaches out from behind the little girl, wrapping round her and pulling her back. Other mothers let their children touch the bones, and one boy walks away with a jaw fragment. As the crowd thins, Venado and Blue-ish tear into their tortillas full of cheese, pepperoni, and mayonnaise lifted from the condiment tables of convenience stores and fast-food restaurants.

The kids want to go up the spindly steel tower, but sightseers plug the stairway and I nix the idea. We leave the tourists on the mountain and descend to Stratton Pond Shelter, where we have to pay. We never heard of it. Pay?

"Five dollars per person," the shelter watchdog tells us.

"I don't have any cash," I tell her.

"I can write you a bill and you can mail the money to the Green Mountain Club," she says.

We fill out the details and she hands me a yellow copy with the particulars.

"Do many people pay these?" I ask.

"No."

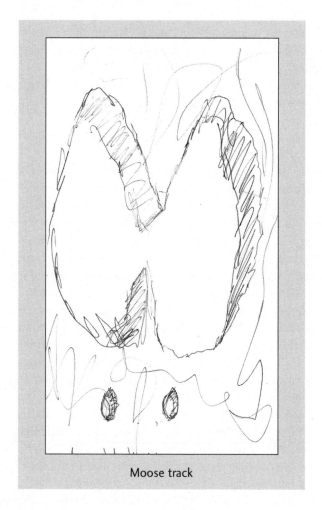

Moose track

"I will."

She shrugs. "We'll see."

"I'll pay it," I assure her, tucking the note into my wallet. "It's part of my religion."

She looks me in the eye and we smile. She asks questions about the kids. "What will you do if you don't finish before school starts?"

"We're homeschooled," the kids interject, almost in unison.

"This *is* school," I tell her, and among other things, Venado and I recite the litany for her. Almost two thousand miles now and we can still name every camp, although he has to cover the northern Virginia section he did with his mom. He has tried to teach it to me, but I have no images to attach the shelter names to.

After some more small talk, the caretaker heads back to her camp.

"That's the most I ever heard her say to anybody," says a guy in the shelter.

"You should travel with kids," I tell him. "People like talking to us."

When last seen, the trails of Vermont offered us mud, snow, moose tracks, moose scat, and the smells of fir and spruce—all signs of home. Three months later, it's summer. The grays and whites of late winter have shifted to lush green, but the moose turds, northern forest smells, and mud remain. "Welcome to Vermud," one hiker we meet says.

Two days out we come across a gang of young folks cutting logs in the forest. We stop to watch as a guy with a bandana tied round his head and a wisp of a beard sprouting from his chin coaches a crew of college-age people on how to move a ten-foot-long, ten-inch-diameter log down onto the trail. They loop slings over both ends of the log and twist them up tight with stout branches, each about four feet long. With one of the crew on each end of the branches, they lift the log between them and start to plow through the brush and saplings. Venado, Blue-ish, and I dodge out of the way as the log bearers charge past us like a bull moose, and we turn to watch them moving briskly down the trail. Further on, we walk on new boardwalks of fresh-cut logs over a particularly muddy stretch of trail.

A day later we meet a crew tearing apart a shelter in the rain.

"What the . . . ?"

Blue-ish and Venado stare openmouthed at the destruction. A young woman in shorts and a rain jacket, her hair matted with rain, sweat, and dirt, comes along the trail, and we ask her what is going on. "We're taking it apart and moving it to a new location," she says.

"Why?"

"It's having too much impact on this area."

We have to speculate what impacts the shelter creates: too much trampling of the trail, destroying flora, making mud, or polluting the nearby lake. We know for certain that thousands of feet walking the same path *do* create impacts, particularly on Vermont's fragile terrain.

For a quarter mile, we meet people carrying pieces of wood along the trail or heading back to the toppled shelter for another load.

What becomes apparent in Vermont—we had seen it elsewhere but not so clearly—is the volunteer work that goes into maintaining the physical trail. Many sections of Vermont would quickly become impassable mud wallows if not for crews of young folks from various hiking clubs coming out for scant pay and rebuilding the vital system of boardwalks. Usually the volunteers are students in need of summer jobs. Groups of a half dozen or so live together in tent camps for weeks or months at a time. They joyfully carry heavy tools for miles through the woods, and get sweaty and bug bitten building whatever needs building: boardwalks, ditches, rock steps, privies, and shelters. They even shovel out the privies!

We often stop to ask the volunteers about their work. "Thanks for coming out here and keeping the trail nice for us," I usually say to them and explain to my children how important these folks are to the trail. "There's nothing else like this," I tell them. "Two thousand miles of trail maintained by volunteers for us to use for free."

At this stage, thru-hikers have thinned out and spread out; those we meet can smell Katahdin only a month away. Most of them have slept next to all sorts of people in the past months and the novelty of making new friends has worn thin. For the most part, they just want to get this thing done. The camaraderie and ease of the south gives way to a sense of urgency. Thru-hikers pass us quickly, racking up twenty to thirty miles a day while we shoot for our steady fifteen. Between our short legs and frequent education stops, big miles are not an option for us. We calculate that Venado will take at least six million steps to finish the trail, a couple million more than the average.

A pair of southbounders tell us about a secret shelter, the location of which can be learned only by word of mouth from certain fellow thru-hikers. "Think about who you pass this information on to," says one of the guys. But elsewhere we find directions in a shelter log.

At a water pump, we meet a young couple that has hiked from Georgia. "Funny, I don't recall your names from the registers," I mention.

"We don't touch the registers," says the woman. "They are the biggest source of germs on the trail."

"Really, like what?"

"Staph," she says.

"Staph?" I ask her. "I never heard of anyone getting staph."

"It's all over the trail," she says.

We get on the subjects of treating water and sanitation. "We seldom treat our water, and we don't bother with hand sanitizer," I admit.

"That's the problem," says the woman.

I don't argue with her, but we continue washing with water only. "I think all that antiseptic stuff is what makes the bacteria stronger," I say to Blue-ish and Venado later.

On the trail people share many things: information, maps, disease, water, time, space, stories, commiseration, sometimes even fuel and food. But up north, after almost two thousand miles, things seem to tighten up.

Late in the season, the north holds more challenges, and we're geared for tougher conditions. Blue-ish wears new boots, Venado is back in his old L.L. Bean boots, and I have switched out my tattered Merrells for the Lowa hiking boots I wore through the mid-Atlantic states back in the winter and spring. "My feet feel better," I tell my kids as autumn approaches. "I can't tell you how much I enjoyed slamming those Merrells into the trash."

After the first week back on the trail, our team slows down. We who had once busted out three eighteen-mile days in a row in Massachusetts can now barely make fifteen miles a day hiking from dawn to dusk, and the days are getting shorter.

"Blue-ish is fine," I tell my wife on a rare cell phone call. "But I get a sense Venado and I are worn out, and my plantar fasciitis is coming back."

"Your *what*?" she asks.

"My sore feet; I found out it's called plantar fasciitis, basically tendonitis of the foot."

When word reaches us about the Long Trail Festival being held in Rutland, just about the time we'll be passing through, we decide to take a zero and connect with our fellow hikers.

In Rutland, we land at a hostel run by an unusual religious group. I recognize the guy running the place, a bearded man in his fifties. "Do you have a house in Boston?" I ask.

"Yeah we do," he says.

"Yeah, I went to one of your feasts once."

"Hopefully, you'll come tonight," the guy tells me, but I beg off.

"It was not that much fun," I tell Blue-ish and Venado privately.

The hostel has separate male and female dorms, and Blue-ish has to go with the women. Venado and I find bunks in the men's quarters, a long room that ends in a row of windows overlooking Rutland's main drag. After showers and laundry, we hit the town, searching for some grub. We end up eating hot dogs and watching the festivities—music and dancing in the streets—but we're too tired for much of that. Venado and Blue-ish drift along like zombies. When I ask what they want to do, they say they'd like to head back to the hostel. Fair enough.

In the morning we eat out again and find our way to the fairgrounds where the festival is getting under way.

It turns into a grand day. GoldenRay, our deaf friend from the south, shows up. Bob Peoples, owner of the Kincora hostel, is there. We make a new friend, an unusual young woman who describes her hike as essentially running away from home. "My parents, my friends all told me I was crazy and that I couldn't do it," she says. "But I love it." She hikes in a skirt and crocs and shuttles her truck along the way. Her trail name, she says, is the nickname her grandfather gave her when she was a little girl: Buttons.

Blue-ish and Venado score all kinds of swag from the vendors: socks, spoons, and mini-Frisbees. I get a gift of Superfeet insoles that soothe my sore feet. Festival organizers request volunteers for trail maintenance the next day, and many of the thru-hikers sign up, but Venado and Blue-ish give the idea a pass. We stay up late listening to music, and camp with our friends at the festival. Next morning, Buttons gives us a ride back to the trailhead and we stop at a convenience store on the way out of town. I offer to buy some packets of Swiss Miss from the coffee bar. "Just take them," the woman behind the counter says and waves us away.

Back on the trail, we find ourselves restored to our element: hiking the miles, often in the rain, eating mac and cheese, and discovering something new every day. We've developed a habit of poking the feathers we find through the ventilation holes in our hats. Now that molting season has arrived, Venado's cap, a black one that says "New York, 1625," has so many feathers sticking out of it that it looks like some sort of war bonnet. He's particularly partial to the black and white wing feathers from the hairy woodpecker and the startling blue, black, and white of the blue jay.

Late one afternoon—two days out of Rutland—Venado, Blue-ish, and I hear many voices off the trail. "We're near Stony Brook," Venado says. "That's where Robin said her son was."

"That's right; what was his name?"

"Silas."

"Yeah, Silas. Let's check it out," I say, and with no path in sight, we stride through the open hardwoods, the three of us spread abreast across a twenty-yard front, heading towards the sound. Walking strong through the forest like that, we look like Mohawks on the scout, striding confident and relaxed into a camp of white kids. But it's all smiles when we break out of the trees, cross a small stream, and find Robin's son Silas and his friends in the midst of a watermelon feast. We introduce ourselves, but his mother has already sent word about us, and he knows who we are. The volunteers welcome us and ply us with sweet, cool melon. They invite us to share the camp, but while we enjoy the feast and company, camping in low country does not appeal to us, and we set off before dark to camp on higher ground, away from the mosquitoes.

GoldenRay catches up with us the next day, and by the time we reach Highway 12, way behind schedule, rain and thunder let loose from above. Taking shelter in a barn alongside the road, we watch as the owner comes out of his house and waves us over to his porch. He greets us with a smile and tells us it's okay to sleep in the barn if we want, and then he invites us in for a meal. We'd already eaten a strawberry-rhubarb pie from a farmer's market down the road, and we stay up way too late filling our bellies with bread and pasta. The barn smells of tractor grease, old hay, and pigeon shit—just like my grandparents' barn, I tell the kids. We lay down our pads and sleeping bags on the dry wooden floor of the third story.

At dawn, we pack up and head for the New Hampshire border, but by the time we've hiked the six miles to Thistle Hill Shelter, where we had planned to have lunch, Venado is singing the blues. "My tummy hurts," he tells us. I feel his forehead. "Not good, you're burning up."

"Can we stay here?"

"Sure. I don't think we have a choice."

Sick boy

We set up a tent in the shelter and Venado collapses inside it, virtually comatose. GoldenRay and Blue-ish and I debate our options as the afternoon wears on.

"I hope it's not Lyme," I write in a note to GoldenRay.

"Do you want me to baby-sit while you go get help?" GoldenRay writes back.

I shake my head.

Blue-ish unpacks the stove. "Do you want me to make lunch, Daddy?"

"Yeah, make some soup for your brother, if you will."

GoldenRay, reading the shelter log, starts tapping the page and speaking, which he seldom does. He slides over to where I sit at the edge of the shelter and shows me the logbook. It contains a phone number for a trail angel in nearby Lebanon, New Hampshire.

"Very good. Let's give this a try." I fish the cell phone out of Blue-ish's pack and dial the number. It's a go; a thru-hiker who finished the week before and her mother will meet us the next morning at a road two miles away.

Come morning, Venado feels a little better. Blue-ish and I lighten his load until he's carrying little more than his clothes and sleeping bag, and we head for the road.

"Poppy?"

"Yes?"

"Do you need a passport to travel between continents?"

"You need a passport to travel between countries, and countries are on continents."

"What about Australia?"

"Yeah, that's a country and a continent. You need a passport," I say as we walk along—me trying to send a text message to the trail angels.

"What about Antarctica?"

"Hmmm. I don't know about that. You might not need a passport to get there, but you would need one to get home."

After a visit to the hospital and a Lyme disease test, the trail angels take us to their home. "Stay as long as you like," they say, and so we relax, watching movies and resting. The trail angels' son is still out on the trail, having contracted Lyme in Pennsylvania. They say that from what they heard, seven percent of the 2010 thru-hikers have already fallen ill with Lyme, and the season is far from over.

The Lyme test comes back negative on the third day, but Venado lobbies for more rest, so we spend another night. "I think he's coming around," I tell my wife on the phone. "But if he fades like this again we're going to have to get off the trail for a while. They weighed him at the hospital and he's fifty-three and three-quarters pounds."

Mrs. Trail Angel takes Blue-ish and Venado to a playground, and later, over dinner, Mr. Trail Angel tells us a story of when he put the cat in the dryer. "I heard something flopping around in there and I stopped the dryer. She was pretty dizzy when I got her out. She stumbled around

"He don't bite."

panting, but she made it." Next morning, they give us a ride back into Vermont, and we head out for a short hike to Happy Hill.

We love the beautiful stone shelter, but that night two rough-looking guys come in and let their dog run wild in the shelter, spilling one hiker's food and snarling and barking viciously at two other guys who come in after dark. "He don't bite," the dog's owner says, making no attempt to restrain his pet. To my children's embarrassment, I tell the guy he needs to leash his dog.

We beat it out of there before sunrise the following morn, but two miles out from the shelter Venado asks, "Papa did you pack my pants?"

"That's your job," I tell him, and we immediately realize that he has forgotten his winter pants, which had been drying by the fire.

"I saw them there," says Blue-ish.

"Why didn't you say something?" I ask.

"We can get new," Venado says.

"No, we cannot," I tell him.

"But we can't go all the way back there."

"Yes, we can, and we will. You need those pants for the Whites."

We stash our packs and hoof it back to the shelter, passing the nasty dog en route. Venado casts a worried look at me. "Don't say anything, Papa, please."

We retrieve the precious pants and head for the Vermont-New Hampshire border. Just into New Hampshire, the trail passes through Hanover, where we stop for pizza and meet a man who gives the kids AT patches for their packs. A couple of miles north of town we pass a side trail to a shelter where we have heard there is some trail magic.

"Shall we check it out?"

"Yeah."

"Yeah."

We hike to a beautiful shelter with a clear Plexiglas roof, and there sits a donut box. Blue-ish opens it and pulls out a chocolate-covered donut. "There's two more," she says.

"Perfect."

We eat up and make a run for it.

"Supposed to rain. We need to get to Moose Mountain," I tell the kids. "We've got to hike hard."

Low on water, we filter from a seep on the way up the mountain and make it to the shelter at dark. No sooner do we get under cover than the pitter patter begins on the roof, and in minutes the sky opens up. The gang at Moose Mountain makes jokes and we tease each other in a way that reminds me of the South. Everyone there seems to have a story about the bad dog.

When day breaks Venado notices a pair of boots full of water, sitting by the fire pit. "Somebody left their boots out in the rain," he says. One of our shelter mates rolls over and looks out. "Oh no," he groans.

13

THE RAIN AND THE PAIN

Approaching Mount Moosilauke, the first of the big mountains, Blue-ish, Venado, and I hear a warning from a veteren thru-hiker: "When you reach the Whites you've completed eighty percent of the trail and twenty percent of the work," he tells us. "It all depends on the weather," he adds, and now the weather turns against us. It had rained and drizzled ever since Moose Mountain, and we'd shared the last shelter with some frat boys who liked to pee right out the opening onto the steps.

"What ails you?" I'd snapped at one, and he'd quickly put himself back together, mumbling excuses.

Bad dogs and bad boys come with the territory, and I remind myself every day how lucky I am to be out here. But I have left MacKaye's book behind on this final leg of the hike. I can see the end in sight, and philosophizing takes a backseat to getting to Katahdin.

Cruising along on a cool autumnal day under scattered clouds, we break out into an opening and find ourselves looking at a ski lift and a grassy ski slope without a white blaze in sight. "We're lost," Blue-ish confirms, and she leads the way back until we find where we missed a turn.

From the beginning, Blue-ish had never expressed enthusiasm for the trail—she had been forced to come along. The fact that, pound for pound, she can carry more and hike faster than Venado and I, or that she can make and break camp without any fuss and hold the trail, does not make her love being out here with us. But the White Mountains bring out the best in her.

As I try not to turn into one of those grim almost-done hikers and Venado's pace slows—he still has the spirit, but his body has reached its limits—Blue-ish charges up the steep slopes, often pivoting to stare down at us with an impatient air of superiority.

She has had that air since birth; the Whites give it expression. She finds them worthy of her interest. I had initially worried that the Whites would intimidate her, but that is hardly the case. Her feet and hands on the granite mountains put life into her. She rocks the Whites, and they rock her.

We cross Cape Moonshine Road around midafternoon. I hold the guidebook open and announce: "It says here that there is an intentional community three quarters of a mile up this road." Venado and Blue-ish look at me. "Should we go there?" I ask. "Might be some kids around."

"Yeah, yeah," they say, and we take a detour to Dancing Bones, a group of half a dozen families living more or less communally on several hundred acres of New Hampshire forest land. The community offers free showers, camping, and cooking facilities for thru-hikers.

Walking along the road as the clouds tear apart and give way to some late-afternoon sun, Venado and Blue-ish seem infused with new energy. They laugh and giggle, and it's me who keeps wondering out loud when we will get there. "This sure seems like more than three quarters of a mile."

We eventually reach a gate with "Dancing Bones" written over it and hike up the long driveway to what appears to be the communal kitchen. We're hanging around wondering what the program is when a woman in a white car pulls up.

"Are you guys hiking the trail?" she asks.

We nod yes.

"Make yourselves at home."

"Anything we need to know about the showers and stuff?"

"We just ask that you not shower too long. Other than that, everything is pretty self-explanatory, and there is a note on the wall there for hikers."

We read the note about the showers, where to cook, to not eat the residents' food, and so on. After the intense religious commune in Rutland, with its strict rules, Dancing Bones offers a very laid-back atmosphere. We are going about our business when a woman shows up with two little boys, one of them, Quinn, a year older than Venado and a year younger than Blue-ish, the other a toddler. The kids hit it right off, and within an hour Venado and Blue-ish shanghai Quinn to hike with us the following day, a Sunday.

"It's only eight miles," I tell Quinn's father, Chip, who agrees to slack-pack us—drive our bags to the Hostel at Glencliff at the foot of Moosilauke. "We have a resupply package there that we can't get until Monday morning," I explain. "So we have to go slow."

"I'll tell you what," Chip says, "how about if I bring you all back here after the hike and I'll take you back to Glencliff Monday morning? That way the kids can play more."

We agree, and next day we take off with Quinn, who we rename *Hablador*—one who never stops talking. The kids jabber about everything from homeschooling to whether Taylor Swift songs are stupid.

"Yes, they are stupid," Hablador says. "But if you like them then they're okay."

When we stop for a snack we learn that Hablador doesn't like walnuts.

"They give you energy," Venado tells him.

"Okay, give me some walnuts."

In Glencliff, Chip shows up and we proceed back to Dancing Bones for another night of play and feasting. Long after dark, I find Venado and Quinn squirreled away in a playroom, building battleships with Legos.

"Come on guys, it's way past our bedtime."

Next morning, we take on the 4,802-foot Mt. Moosilauke, and by lunchtime we make the summit. The sun shines on hikers lounging around barefoot, as if at the beach. To the northeast rises the formidable massif of the Presidential Range; the naked tops of the gray mountains, jagged against a deep blue sky, appear rougher than anything we have seen. After a summer picnic on the windless summit of Moosilaukee, we make it down to Beaver Brook just ahead of a big family, and we pack twelve people into an eight-person shelter. The next morning we make a stop in Woodstock to augment our supplies, and we pitch our tent that evening with some old friends at Eliza Brook.

In the night, the kids awaken to me fussing out in the dark. "Ouch ouch ajeezish . . . "

"What is it?" they ask me.

"Urrrrr." I stumble back into the tent. "I got up to pee and didn't put my crocs on and stepped on a sharp rock—*ahhhgggg*." Flashlight in my teeth, I inspect the deep cut in the arch of my already-aching foot. Blue-ish leans over my shoulder mumbling some commiseration.

In the morning we get ready to hike on. People who had night hiked lie around the fire pit in sleeping bags covered with a thin glimmer of frost. Blue-ish and Venado watch me swallow a couple of ibuprofen before we all hike down the mountain to Lonesome Lake, the first of the Appalachian Mountain Club huts.

After a long descent, we come out of the woods to find a lodge of sorts, a well-made wooden building with lightly laden day-hikers milling in and out. A few thru-hiker packs sit outside, easily distinguishable by a worn look that we all share. Having come this far, all our gear looks familiar: the crocs and the sleeping pads and the water bottles hanging from our light packs are all scuffed and scratched—like us. We're thin, and most of the men have full beards—and we smell wild, like wind and earth, rather than the scented laundry detergent that identifies day-hikers.

Venado, Blue-ish, and I look around, trying to get our bearings and figure out what to do next. "I smell food up there," says Blue-ish, and we follow her up into a dining room. On a table stands an array of hot drinks and soups for sale. I pull a few bills from my pocket and count them. "Looks like we can afford a hot drink and a soup each," I say, and start to pour myself a coffee. Blue-ish and Venado empty packets of Swiss Miss and marshmallows into big ceramic cups and fill them with hot water.

"Ya gotta admit, this ain't bad."

"Poppy, can we stay here and do work for stay?"

"I don't know, let's ask and see if it's an option."

But the hut "croo," as they're called, mostly white kids from various universities, practically give us the bum's rush when we ask.

"It's too early. You need to keep hiking," says a young woman from behind the counter. She turns away abruptly and disappears into the kitchen.

"I guess we keep hiking."

We cross a valley, Franconia Notch, and head up the side of a ridge, using all fours to reach Liberty Springs Campsite, at 3,870 feet.

"Why do we have to camp here?" Venado asks.

"In the Whites we have to stay at a hut or campsite, no stealth camping."

"Why can't we stay at a hut?

"Because it costs something like a hundred dollars apiece. That would pretty much destroy our budget, which I don't even want to think about anymore." Seaweed had sent an email a few days before: *Stop spending money!*

We can smell the campground before we get there, a mix of fermented urine, laundry soap, and bug spray. Under the canopy of dark spruces, colorful tents cover almost every platform. The kids and I look around, but before we can make a choice, the camp caretaker shows up.

"We're pretty full tonight," he tells us.

"We're thru-hikers," I tell him.

"Are you the Barbarians?"

We nod.

"I heard about you. Sure, I think you can squeeze onto platform ten. And we'll waive the fee."

"Thanks."

He points us in the direction of the platform, down a trail along a steep slope covered with spruce.

"It's supposed to rain tonight," he calls as we walk away.

While the kids pitch the tent, I set up our tarp like an awning over a relatively flat spot among the spruces.

"What are you doing that for?" Blue-ish wants to know.

Papa in poncho

"This'll be our staging area if it's raining tomorrow."

Two tents barely fit on platform ten, and the one we share it with is full of heavyweights who, every time they roll over, bounce the kids and me up in the air. We wake up in a downpour. Heavy clouds mask the faint light of dawn on a north slope, and we lie in our bags, listening to the storm. With no alternative, we eat breakfast in our gloomy tent and then go through the difficult task of breaking camp in the rain, with me directing the procedure and gradually moving packed gear from the tent to under the tarp, where we try to keep it as dry as possible. "Sure glad we put up this tarp, eh?" Standing there in our ponchos, we strike the tarp last; I strap the soaked mess to my pack and we head up the mountain.

Trickles run down the rocks, the forest litter soaks up the rain like a giant sponge, and our boots alternate between squishing in sodden mulch and slipping on the wet granite.

"Going up, you have four points of contact," I say. "But going down, it's five points of contact: hands, feet, and butt."

The kids laugh. But things get serious as we approach the tree line and feel the full force of the wind. Blue-ish and Venado have lashed trash bags over their packs. Venado, who lost his poncho in Vermont, wears my rain jacket and I am stuck using a cheap emergency poncho we bought at the dollar store in Brattleboro.

Blowing near fifty miles per hour, the wind hits us hard on the approach to Mounts Lincoln and Lafayette. Our flimsy rain covers and ponchos slap and flap with such a nerve-racking riot we can hardly talk.

"Maybe we should go around the summit, avoid this wind," I shout as the rain pelts my face.

"No!" the kids shout back.

"White blazes!" calls Venado, and they climb out of earshot, following the well-worn path. A post with a battered sign on Mount Lincoln marks the summit of our first five-thousand-footer since the south. We look around, squinting into the clouds.

"Some nice view," I shout over the staccato slapping of wet plastic. "I think I see the Eiffel Tower over there."

"Yeah, there's Mount Everest," say Venado.

"Come on, let's get out of here," Blue-ish says, and that makes sense to us.

After we make it over the equally inhospitable Mount Lafayette, the trail turns downhill and the wind is at our backs. In less than a mile, we reach the tree line and some relief. The rain slacks off to a heavy drizzle as we follow a side trail to the Garfield Ridge Shelter. Along the way, a sign points to a scenic view shrouded in clouds; we laugh and head straight for the shelter.

"Goddangit I'm cold," I say, stripping off wet gear. Blue-ish and Venado have fared better in their ponchos and leggings. Blue-ish takes the lunch fixings from me while I focus on getting into dry pants, setting aside for later my spare socks and the linen shirt I have carried since day one. Sitting on the messy deck of the shelter, I peel the bandage off my foot to let the suppurating wound air out.

"Poppy, your foot looks gross," says Venado.

"Yeah," I say, jamming antibacterial ointment into the pit of raw meat. "Just lucky it's in the arch, or I'd be outta business."

Blue-ish hands me a tortilla. "How far are we going today, Daddy?" she asks.

"Galehead Hut, I hope. We'll have to see if we can get a work for stay."

"How far is that?"

"Check the book. Do the math."

Blue-ish takes the book from me and after a minute she hands it back.

After bolting our tortillas and cramming our mouths full of gorp, we put on wet socks and boot up. "I love that feeling of water squishing between my toes when I stand up," I say.

"Where's my rain jacket?" Venado asks.

"Where'd you leave it?"

"Here." Venado touches the nail where he hung his wet jacket.

"Is that it in the puddle?" Blue-ish says, nodding at his now wet *and* muddy jacket lying on the ground.

Coming out of Garfield, the trail drops in a four-hundred-foot freefall to an alpine valley below. It's slow going, full of strenuous moves over slanted ledges that threaten to take us on uncontrolled slides. Leaning back to avoid the nasty prospect of a forward fall, we often lose our footing and drop onto our butts.

"How far from Garfield to Galehead, Blue-ish?"

"Two point seven miles, mostly downhill."

"Woohooo!" I shout.

After two more hours in a steady drizzle, we start to meet day-hikers from the hut and descend with them to the lonely outpost. A croo member meets us at the door and tells us to go around to the kitchen and ask the hut master about work for stay. A young guy in shirtsleeves leans out the back door of the lodge, examining us. From under our rain gear we look right past him and into the well-lit kitchen, which effuses rich smells of food.

"You're thru-hikers?" he asks in disbelief.

"Yeah," says Venado, with Blue-ish and I nodding in confirmation.

The hut master continues to give us a skeptical look, but tells us to come through the front door. Inside, we meet several other thru-hikers, all dripping in a corner. The croo leader pops questions at the kids from the kitchen, where he's preparing supper, and they quickly satisfy him that they have come a long way.

"I'm sorry," he says finally. "But I . . . you're the youngest thru-hikers I ever saw." He gives the kids hot chocolate.

I look around the hut, the varnished wood, long tables, and hallways that lead we know not where. "So what's the story?" I ask one of the other thru-hikers, a gray-haired man.

"We wait here until the guests finish eating, then we get whatever is left over and do the dishes or something," he replies in an Australian accent.

"Where do we sleep?"

"On the floor, or the tables. I don't really know."

"Mexicans say it's bad luck to sleep on a table," I tell him. "That's where they wake the dead."

Blue-ish and Venado have changed into their dry or at least less wet gear and begin tearing apart what looks like a hiker box.

"That's the lost and found," one of the croo tells them.

We watch the guests eating, and then chatting over coffee, until finally the croo puts out trays of leftovers and invites us all to eat. The kids dive into warm lasagna, cold garlic bread, and salad. A few of the children among the guests come round to quiz Blue-ish and Venado, and before long the kids have integrated the thru-hikers and the guests.

I answer many questions put to me by a young woman who has come up here every year since she was a child. She invites her aunts to come join us, and I notice the guests beginning to accept us thru-hikers as fellow outdoors lovers. The hut sells kid-sized quick-dry shirts, the first we have seen, and I buy one for Venado. We listen to one of the croo give a lecture on how to cope with lightning at high elevations, and it's near ten o'clock by the time we roll our sleeping bags out on the floor.

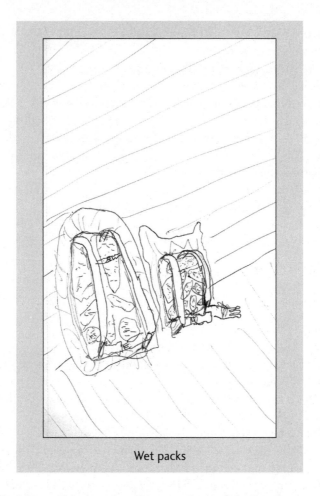

Wet packs

All night we listen to the whirring whine of the wind generator as the gales that give the hut its name scream past the eaves.

By dawn, the wind has died down. The rain dissipates into intermittent clouds of heavy mist, and after breakfast and chores, we depart in the company of Wizard, the Aussie, and his wife, Tripper. "I earn that name the hard way," she says, feigning a stumble.

"How'd you like the hut?" I ask Wizard as we head up the trail.

The gray-bearded hiker shakes his head. "Seemed strange the way they set it up. Elitist."

I nod. "It got better once we got to meet people. I guess if they're paying a hundred bucks a night, we do look a bit like beggars."

Wizard and Tripper hike away from us. "We only have six-month visas," they explain, "and we may not finish."

On a steep climb, we come up behind the young woman who I'd met the night before. Drawing near, we hear her singing beautifully to her aunts. We stop and listen a while before passing them. Up above the tree line again, we come across patches of wild highland cranberries and stop to feast.

"These things are super rich in vitamin C," I say as Blue-ish and Venado graze through a patch.

We eat lunch at Zealand Falls Hut, and when I tell the kids we can't afford soup, another hiker buys soup for them.

"FOG," he says when we ask his name. "Fat Old Guy."

He passes us later on, going over the next mountain.

A light rain returns as the day ends, and we find our destination, Ethan Pond Shelter, packed with weekend hikers. The caretaker comes around and tries to collect eight dollars a head from me, but I take him aside. "We're thru-hikers, and you want to charge twenty-four dollars for us to sleep in this cramped, wet shelter with no water source? Are you serious? The last guy didn't even charge us."

"Who was that?"

"Never mind."

"It was the guy at Liberty, wasn't it?"

"I can't remember now," I say. "What do you want to do?"

After some haggling, we settle on me paying the eight dollars and the kids staying for free. The night goes well; we end up having a sing-along with the weekenders. Next morning breaks clear and sunny, and we make an easy three-mile hike down to Crawford Notch. At the general store, we pick up a resupply box and winter gear. I check my email, and upon learning that our old friend Chutzpah has sent us a hundred fifty dollars, we decide to spend the money on a *nearo*—an almost-zero day.

Consulting the guidebook, we locate the cheapest hotel in the area—it's in Bretton Woods, so we start hitching the ten miles up there. A man and a young boy pick us up. "You guys looked interesting," the man says. "I wanted my son to hear your story." So we share some tales of our adventures with them on the short drive up the valley.

At the motel, the owner gives us free passes to a nearby ski lift and discount coupons for the buffet at a restaurant on top of the mountain. We dump our packs in the room, shower quickly, and head for the free ride up the mountain on a warm sunny day.

Later, bellies full of burgers, potato salad, and other goodies, we call it our best zero ever. "Nearo," Venado reminds us.

Back at the motel, the owners do our laundry for free. We dry our boots in the sun and I nurse my foot. "This is never going to heal with all this rain," I say.

While Blue-ish and Venado watch TV, I work on submitting a job application via iPhone. I tell the kids to leave me alone, but Blue-ish leans over my shoulder and I snap at her. She runs into the bathroom crying and slams the door on me as I follow her, apologizing. After a while we settle down and watch TV together. I've been trying not to become an ogre, but the strain of keeping everything organized and moving gets the best of me at times. I'm starting to remind myself of my father packing the car and preparing us all for our annual vacation to the Jersey Shore; it was never easy.

Our resupply box contains extra Band-Aids, Sno-Seal, and silk liners for the sixty-degree sleeping bags Venado and I are still trying to get away with.

"Are you warm enough with your bag?" I ask Blue-ish.

She shrugs. "Yeah."

The forecast bodes ill for the next day, but it's still clear when we leave the motel. The owners take a picture of us before we go, and the guy who picks us up hitchhiking to the trailhead gives me a twenty-dollar bill as we get out of his truck. We head up 6.4 miles and 3,523 feet toward Mizpah Spring Hut, dry-footed for the first time in days. That happy experience doesn't last an hour before the rain comes and soaks us.

"Oh boy, this is going to be rock scrambling all the way," I say, looking up the steep wet incline.

"I like it," says Blue-ish and as the rain falls harder, soaking through our heavily greased boots, soaking my aching foot, we find ourselves giggling over evil fantasies—like squirting some of the ketchup packets lifted from yesterday's buffet down onto mountain bikers who'd been riding below the ski lift.

We get to Mizpah early in the afternoon, but too late to make it to Lakes of the Clouds. So we do another work for stay and by chance meet a couple of people we know from Maine.

The hut master has the kids set the table and asks me to police the grounds outside the hut. The task seems unusual; not many people litter up here. Outside, I pick up bits of microtrash, like the torn corner of an energy bar wrapper and a piece of plastic broken off someone's hiking pole. I do find a used menstrual pad, probably dropped by accident, and wonder if that's why I've been sent out here. I pick it up, using the plastic bag as a glove, and go back in with the meager bag of trash. After we watch the paying customers eat dinner, the hut master and one of the croo do a skit intended to remind guests to put money in the tip jar. It's a ritual, performed at every hut by the notoriously underpaid staff.

Venado and Blue-ish stand against a wall, smiling at the antics, and afterwards the croo gives Blue-ish a birthday cupcake and the entire hut sings "Happy Birthday" to her on the eve of her turning eleven. She is smitten. "This is my favorite hut," she says. We try to buy her a shirt, but the season is almost over and they are out of her size. "You can get one at Pinkham Notch," one of the croo tells her.

We dry our gear as best we can in the largely unheated hut and sack out in the library. At dawn we put on our damp clothes and beat it out of Mizpah before anyone else. Hiking ahead, Blue-ish stops suddenly. Venado and I catch up and see a spruce grouse on the trail. We watch it walk around, only a few feet from us, and study its gray plumage flecked with startling red and white around the head.

"Come on, we can't stay here all day," I finally say.

We pass more cranberry patches and stop to pick the ripe fruit. For a moment, the clouds part and we see the mountains all around us.

"When you were a baby I made a plan to hike with you in your backpack, but we never pulled it off," I tell Blue-ish. "I was planning to stay at Lakes of the Clouds and Madison with you. Hiking the Whites is something we're long overdue for."

"Really?"

"For real," I say as we make our way down a steep shelf of granite. And as Blue-ish turns away, smiling, I slip and go down hard. It's almost like slow motion. Blue-ish watches wide-eyed as I flail for a hold and fetch up on a sharp rock, right in the ribs.

"Oooooo!"

"Are you okay?"

"No. Oouch," I say, lying there on the wet rock, trying to collect myself.

"Poppy, how come you don't cry when you get hurt?"

"Because I worked on fishing boats for so many years, and crying wasn't appreciated, so I got out of the habit."

The kids wait while I pull myself together. Breathing against the pain in my side, I smile. "Venado, get out the energy bars. Let's take a little break."

Venado opens his pack. "Birthday girl chooses," he says, and spreads an assortment of energy bars in front of his sister. We all focus on which of the precious snacks she'll pick; the tension mounts.

"I choose . . . cookies and cream," Blue-ish decides finally, and she mimes putting a candle in the energy bar. "It's my birthday cake!" Such is the celebration, somewhere up on a fog-bound ridge, way above the tree line in the Whites.

By the time we reach Lakes of the Clouds Hut, at 5,050 feet, the wind has picked up and the mist has thickened to almost rain. We find a dozen thru-hikers bogged down only a mile and a half from the summit of Mount Washington. The croo and guests apparently feel overrun with thru-hikers. We spot Wizard and Tripper sitting down to supper with the paying guests.

I walk over and ask Wizard what's up. "We got tired of the work-for-stay routine so we decided to splurge and get bunks."

That's out of the question for Blue-ish, Venado, and me, so we kill time playing checkers. It gets dark, with the place full and a dozen thru-hikers on hand; we don't see any food until ten, and it's near eleven when the kids finally get in their bags, Venado complaining and running a fever. One of the croo asks if he is okay, and I take her aside.

"Listen, I understand you have a big crowd and the weather's bad, but leaving little kids to wait till ten o'clock to eat just doesn't work for them. They needed to be fed and in bed hours ago."

"Why didn't you say something?" she protests.

"Because I kept thinking any minute things would change."

She apologizes, and I apologize for giving her a hard time.

The Appalachian Mountain Club generally supports thru-hiking and tries to balance the needs of its members with those of the various thru-hikers seeking shelter. The AMC hut at Upper Goose Pond, where we camped on the porch and met Nature Boy, is exclusively for thru-hikers and section hikers, and the other huts' croos often accept more than the two work-for-stay thru-hikers that the AMC recommends. But the relationship isn't always easy.

We sometimes find a degree of tension in the huts—the class consciousness that Wizard noticed—and while we understand that we are not paying customers, it feels odd to be in the United States watching others eat and waiting for the leftovers. When bad weather forces us to rely exclusively on the huts, it doesn't help.

We thru-hikers talk about the situation with varying degrees of acceptance, wishing the Appalachian Trail Conservancy and AMC could provide an option that would enable us to take care of ourselves in bad weather. "They won't let the AMC build any more shelters up here," someone says.

In the morning one of the croo brings the kids hot chocolate. Blue-ish and I watch the anemometer: winds gusting to forty. It's supposed to clear up, but the windchill is below freezing.

"I don't know if we've got the gear to pull this off," I tell the kids. "Venado, how are you feeling? Can you make it a mile and a half?"

"I think so."

"Put on everything you got, you guys. Blue-ish, you take what you can from his pack. Your mom's coming up today. We'll get off the trail for a while and get this boy fattened up."

We put on all our clothes, lighten Venado's pack, and head off into the fog. "It's not so bad. How's everybody doing?" I ask after we pass the lake.

Blue-ish, walking ahead in her blue poncho, the color vibrant in the hazy light, turns and smiles. "Good," she says.

"Okay," says Venado without stopping. The clouds envelop us so thickly that we have no idea where we stand in relation to the summit. Occasionally, we can hear the train on the cog railroad chugging toward the top. When we reach the first sign of civilization, a radio tower, Venado sits down, crying. I offer to carry his pack; mumbling something, he sloughs it off and plods on. I pick up the little pack and lash it to the top of mine. Together, we make our way to the summit and grab pictures at the Mount Washington sign before heading into the restaurant. Wizard and Tripper are there, so is AD, a dreadlocked hiker we'd met in Vermont, and a bunch of other thru-hikers we have hopscotched with since coming into the Whites.

I call Seaweed. "Where are you?" I ask.

"Waiting for you guys. Are you going to hike down? What's the plan?"

"I think we've got a very tired boy on our hands. You better come up and get us." She protests about the cost, but I tell her it's cheaper than the three of us taking the bus down. So she drives up and we throw a party for the other thru-hikers, sharing all the food Seaweed brought thinking we were going to hike together for a couple of days. It's fun to watch AD wolf down a piece of fresh quiche, and afterwards we pile into the Honda Fit and head home to Maine.

"We've got to fatten this boy up if we want to finish the trail," I say. Venado and Blue-ish sit in the backseat, talking over each other to their mom, filling her in on all their adventures, as she drives us all down the mountain.

Two Philosophies, One Trail

From the very beginning we have focused on Benton MacKaye's contribution to the trail, but as we get ready for Maine, we learn more about Myron Avery. In Maine, he is the better-known cocreator of the AT, and shortly after his death in 1952, the Maine legislature voted to rename the east peak of Mount Bigelow "Avery Peak."

MacKaye brought a spiritual, almost metaphysical, perspective to the trail, and a global idealism that, while inspiring for us, never became part of the thru-hiker's ethos. Myron Avery came from Lubec, Maine, a place where one thing earned respect: hard work that produced tangible results. Apparently Avery excelled at that.

A graduate of Bowdoin College and Harvard, Avery was elected chairman of the Appalachian Trail Conference in 1932. He poured his ample energies into surveying and measuring the trail, because, according to one writer: "He believed that the actual existence of an unbroken trail would provide the only guarantee of public use and acceptance of the Appalachian Trail, in both fact and concept."

Described as obsessive and unable "to be associated with an enterprise without running it," Avery insisted that the trail be built, maintained, and marked according to uniform standards, and he rode roughshod over anyone who disagreed. "Myron left two trails," claimed one member of the Potomac Appalachian Trail Club, of which Avery was also president. "One was of hurt feelings and bruised egos, the other was the AT."

What Avery lacked in graciousness he made up for in energy and dedication. His workhorse spirit can be seen more frequently along the trail than MacKaye's idealistic modern Barbarism, and he set the standard for accuracy in trail guide books—and we appreciate that every day. Venado and I put almost complete faith in our *Thru-Hikers' Companion* and it rarely lets us down.

In Maine we often find ourselves using all fours to climb steep rock scrambles. "Old Myron Avery didn't think much of switchbacks, did he?" I quip to one shelter caretaker in western Maine.

"No sah," says the young man with a thick Maine accent. "He figah'd if you was goin' up, you might as well go straight up."

As the first person to hike every mile of the trail (in sections, over ten years), Avery became the architect of the thru-hike, and his relentless drive to build the trail all the way from Georgia to Katahdin gets rekindled every spring by thousands of hikers setting off from one end of the trail or the other—or in our case, the middle. ■

14

MAINE

At home, we go barefoot. I grill our homemade lamb sausage and juicy steaks from Tide Mill Farm, fifteen miles down the road. We splurge on ice cream and pie—everything's on the menu. While Venado may be walking on little man legs, muscular and toned, we need to put meat and fat on his all-too-visible ribs. The blueberry fields that carpet our region are heavy with ripe fruit and we bury pancakes under mountains of fresh blueberries, make blueberry smoothies, and eat berries by the warm handful. After eleven days of gluttony, Venado tips the scale at fifty-eight pounds, and if we want to get to Katahdin before Baxter Park closes on October 15, we have to go. I had once envisioned finishing in late August, but now we are cutting it pretty close.

We head back to New Hampshire as a family, and the logistics get a little complex when we have to stealth-camp on the side of a mountain. Seaweed, Venado, and Blue-ish brave a rainy, cold night huddled together in their summer bags in one tent on the only flat spot. I sleep alone in our little tent, trying to find the comfort zone on top of a root. Venado and I had decided to do a thirty-six mile southbound section

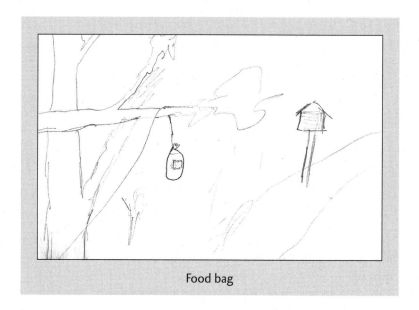

Food bag

from Route 2 near Gorham back to Mount Washington, and then hitch back to Route 2 and continue north.

"You sure you don't want to call it good—head north from here?" I'd asked Venado as we'd prepared to head south. "I'm kinda sick of negotiating these AMC huts."

He had looked up at me. "What? No. That would be cheating."

"Okay, okay." We had parked at the trailhead east of Gorham and headed south for the first time since we'd been on the trail.

After our one rainy night together on rough ground, Seaweed and Blue-ish circle back to the car, leaving Venado and me on a course for Mount Washington, which we're duty-bound to climb a second time.

We plug on through more rain. "Remember Giant?" I ask.

"Yeah, he didn't think we'd make it."

"Yeah, what an attitude. I haven't heard anything about him in a while. I wonder if he's still even on the trail."

One of those amazing things: The next person we see coming towards us on the trail stands well over six feet tall and looks hauntingly familiar.

"Hey, it's the Barbarians," the approaching hiker says.

"Giant? Wow! We were just talking trash about you half a mile back." I drop my pack and give him an awkward hug.

Venado smiles. "We thought you were gone."

"No. I'm still here," says Giant in his nonchalant way. But he is pale and shivering.

"You look a bit peaked," I say. "You okay?"

"I'm okay. I just need to keep moving." Giant's hiking buddy, a young woman named DB, comes down the hill behind him, and he introduces her as she joins us. Like Giant, she keeps her pack on, ready to go, but we keep extending the conversation.

"We're about to cook lunch. Sit down," I say.

"Oh what the hell," he says and finally drops his pack. "You can hike on, I'll catch up," he says to DB and she waves and continues up the trail.

Giant gets out his cook gear and dumps two packs of ramen into a pot.

"Still running on ramen and Pop-Tarts?" I ask.

"All the way."

"Geez. I don't know how you do it."

Venado and I eat our pepperoni and cheese tortillas and organic ramen.

"We just got back on the trail," Venado tells Giant, filling him in on our adventures.

Giant and I trade notes on the rest of our ever-expanding hiking family.

"I talked to Dos XX in July; he was in PA, laid up with plantar fasciitis."

"I hear Watermelon got Lyme," says Giant. "I haven't seen many people since I left you guys in Virginia."

"Yeah, you killed Popeye. He got off on Roan Mountain, but I keep in touch with him on Facebook. I miss him."

Giant shrugs, still shivering a bit.

"You oughta take a break," I suggest. "Get yourself together for Maine."

We carp together about the huts. Giant warns us about Madison Spring Hut. "They turned a bunch of us away in the rain, near dark,"

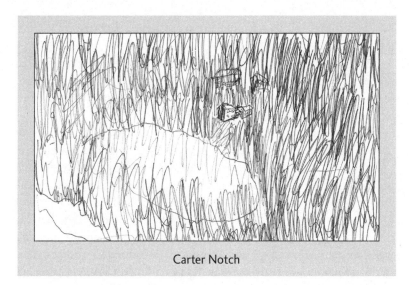

Carter Notch

he tells us. "Try not to get stuck there." We head off in separate directions, and at midafternoon, Venado spots Carter Notch Hut down in a rainy valley. We descend toward the buildings, which stand dark and wet around a small pond; smoke emanates from a chimney above the largest building and we slip quietly in, planning to enjoy a hot snack and then hike on. But the croo takes an interest in us.

"You guys thru-hiking?" a young woman asks.

I shrug, but Venado lets the cat out of the bag. "Yeah!"

"How'd you know?" I ask her.

"We heard about a little guy with lots of feathers in his hat," she says nodding toward Venado's well-adorned cap. "Do you guys want to do work for stay?"

I explain, diplomatically, why work for stay doesn't work for us, but she says we can eat with the guests and have our own bunks, and so we agree. "As long as we can get out at the crack of dawn, Venado."

"Okay."

To Venado's delight, he actually gets a job. "Finally, we get to a place that actually gives us work," says Venado, as he and I vigorously scrub pots for an hour. Later a family arrives with a young boy, and he and Venado enjoy some play time. Before we leave in the morning, I buy Venado a polar fleece hat. "I think it's time for this." Venado puts it on over his cap the way I wear mine, but it crushes his feathers, so he takes the cap off and ties it to his pack.

We make it over Wildcat Mountain in clearing weather, hike through Pinkham Notch, and camp at the foot of Mount Madison, ready to summit Mount Washington the following day. "Supposed to be good weather."

The sun rises with us hiking, and the air is so still we can smell a guy smoking a cigarette a quarter mile away. We pass him and head up the mountain on a clear and nearly windless day. All morning we watch a helicopter lifting a cargo net full of building materials up to the mountaintop and returning with a net full of debris. People we meet coming down tell us that the AMC has begun to demolish Madison Spring Hut in preparation for rebuilding it. We find only the kitchen left standing when we get there, and we stop for water. A construction worker invites us in and points us toward the sink. As I'm filling the last bottle, one of the croo comes in and gives us a harsh look. "Can I help you!" It's not really a question, but I smile.

"We're all set now, thanks." And we run out the door laughing. "Thru-hikers must have been hard on her," I say to Venado.

Outside, we get an up-close view of the helicopter we have been watching all morning. It hovers above as a worker unhooks the net full of lumber and hooks up a net full of broken timbers and shingles. I pull Venado back. "Let's not stand right under it, eh?"

On a spectacular hike around the rim of the Great Gulf, a steep glacial hollow ten miles wide, we pass numerous groups carrying flags up the peaks along the way. One group reminds us that it's September 11, and they explain that they plan to put flags on all the highest peaks. We have our own goal, and we go boulder hopping across the barren mountaintops from Madison to Washington, with sunshine and views for hundreds of miles.

Late in the afternoon, tired, we slog up the last quarter mile toward the summit of Mount Washington. The cog train goes by, and we look at tourists looking back us. We touch the "Mt Washington, 6,288 ft." sign again, and hitch a ride down off the mountain with a family from India. I ask where in India they are from.

"Kerala," says the woman. "Trivandrum. Are you familiar with India?"

Mama moose and two calves

"We lived in Trivandrum," Venado says, smiling in surprise.

"This linen shirt was made in Trivandrum," I tell them tugging on my sleeve for emphasis. We share stories about India all the way down the mountain.

At Pinkham Notch a good-hearted man gives us a break on the price of an all-you-can-eat dinner and we chow down. Camping in the woods across the road from the lodge, we wake up in the middle of the night to a loud splashing nearby, something big. I fumble for our flashlight and shine it out in time to illuminate a cow moose and two calves emerging from a brook and climbing past our camp.

"Papa, did you see that?!"

"How could I not?"

The next day, we find the tracks and follow them into the woods for a few yards before returning to the road to hitch a ride back up to Gorham. After a stop at a 7-Eleven for more energy bars, we return to the trailhead where we started our brief southbound journey, and head for Maine. Venado has switched to a forty-degree down sleeping bag, but with night temperatures still in the fifties, I try to get by with my sixty-degree bag and a silk liner.

We cross the Maine state line the next day on a wet and muddy trail, rain in the forecast, everything wet. A cardboard sign lying in the mud under the boundary marker reads: "Look Ma, I made it to Maine." Venado picks it up and I take his picture. We make it to Carlo Col and camp in a crowded shelter with some of the stinkiest socks on the trail. But nobody cares. When one guy sprays antifungal spray into his boots, filling the shelter with the aerosol mist, people tease him that they will not have to worry about fungus growing in their lungs.

As usual, Venado and I depart before everyone else. There is a cold bite in the air, and we hike a couple of miles to warm our bodies before making breakfast.

We arrive ahead of the pack at the next shelter and score a bag of five Twix candy bars. They are squished but edible, and we tear into them.

"Poppy, what did you do with that fifth one?"

"I don't know. Maybe I gave it away."

"Did you eat it?"

"Um . . . yeah."

Venado accuses me of being unfair.

"I couldn't help it—you got plenty," I tell him. "Besides, I carry most of the food." We pack up and follow the path out of the shelter; it leads down across a ravine, and as we begin climbing up the other side, we hear a shout from behind us.

"Barbarians!"

Back near the shelter stands Spoon, with Joker, Watermelon, and another guy we haven't met yet.

"Spoon! Hey hey!" We wait for our old friends to cross the ravine and we have a big reunion. Everyone's hair is longer, and with the exception of Venado our beards are thicker, but we recognize each other. The new guy's name is Zamboni, because he used to drive one of those big machines used to groom ice-skating rinks.

"Where you heading today?" they ask us.

"We're gonna do Mahoosuc Notch and hopefully get to Speck Pond," we tell them.

"Us too."

"See you there."

Spoon and his gang take off, disappearing ahead.

"They say Mahoosuc Notch is the hardest mile on the AT, Venado."

"Cool."

We enter the notch and clamber over, under, and around the incredible jumble of fallen boulders. The massive chunks of granite lie piled in the steep-sided ravine like giant cookie crumbs fallen into the crease of a sofa. We pass our packs ahead of us through narrow passages under megaliths of granite. Arriving at the foot of the trail to Speck Pond, we check the time. It has taken us a little more than an hour to go one mile, but that's not too bad; from what we've heard it can take much longer. But the sun has set when we get to Speck Pond, and we make camp in the last bit of twilight. The gang has all settled into their winter sleeping bags.

"Supposed to go down into the twenties," somebody says. Venado and I cook our supper by flashlight and turn in, me wearing everything I've got as I climb into my flimsy bag.

Sometime in the dark, Venado rolls over.

"You warm?" I ask.

"Um, sort of. Are you?"

"Not at all."

Next morning, I talk about being on the edge of shivering all night. "I just kept trying to relax and think warm thoughts."

"Warm thoughts," repeats Joker, laughing.

We hike together down into Grafton Notch and, standing around a parking lot on a crisp autumn morning, we all debate our next moves. Venado and I have to pick up a resupply box at Mahoosuc Mountain Lodge, and everyone decides to join us for a zero.

"Nearo," Venado reminds us.

We call the lodge and ask for a shuttle. When the guy arrives with a van to pick us up, I look at him closely.

"Do I know you?"

The driver looks at me a second. "I think we met at the Common Ground fair," he says. "My wife and I do a demonstration there every year."

"That's right, that's it."

It turns out his name is Kevin Slater and he has sled dogs and makes Ojibwa-style snowshoes similar to the type I used to make. We

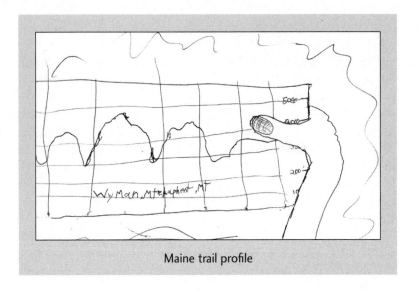

Maine trail profile

hit it off like old times and Kevin tells us we can use his farm truck to go into town. At the lodge, he puts me in charge of the woodstove. "I figure you know what you're doing," he says.

Spoon, Watermelon, Joker, and Zamboni want to go out for a few beers, so they take a shuttle into town while Venado and I take the old truck in and knock around on our own.

Later, back at the lodge, we spend the evening reading Kevin's many books on native crafts and watching a video: *Jurassic Park.* In the morning, I wake up to the sound of a howling sled-dog chorus.

"I haven't heard that since I had my own little team back twenty years ago," I tell Venado as we build a fire in the cookstove. Venado and I eat the farm eggs, local bacon, and raw milk we bought at village markets, while the other guys pour big bowls full of boxed cereal that they eat cold. "We stopped at one little store," I tell them, "and the woman said Venado could have a free cookie if I could tell her how to say 'goodbye' in Italian."

"*Arrivederci,*" says Spoon.

"Give the man a cookie."

We put clean clothes on our clean bodies and load up our gear. Venado and I lift our packs and groan. "Poppy, my pack is heavy."

"Tell me about it."

"What's up, you guys?" Joker asks.

"We're packing six days of food, just to see what it will be like in the 100-Mile Wilderness," I tell him. "It's obvious we're going to have to figure something else out."

Kevin loans me an arctic-rated sleeping bag liner. "Just mail it back to me when you're done," he says.

The heavy-duty liner adds another two pounds to my pack, and on the climb out of Grafton Notch, Spoon and company leave us far behind. As usual in Maine, the trail goes straight up and straight down every mountain.

I make up a song, off-key and out of time:

"Oh, Myron Avery, you make the trail so steep, just like we knew you would. And you make us climb them up and down because you knew we could."

Venado learns it and starts adding his own verses: "Oh, Myron Avery, you never heard of a switchback . . . " But by the time we slip and slide down the north side of Baldpate Mountain we've forgotten it all. At Frye Notch Lean-to, I hand Venado a heaping bowl of mac and cheese.

"Poppy, I can't eat all this."

"Well, do what you can. I sure can't carry it."

I pile on the food like never before. "We don't want you losing weight again," I say, but by the time we reach the camp at Little Swift River Pond we have eaten so much we won't make it to our next resupply.

"Poppy, there are canoes down at the pond," Venado reports after exploring the area. "Can we go fishing?"

"Sure. Find some bait."

We share the camp with two other hikers, Country Gold, heading south, and Slightly Inappropriate, heading north. Country Gold tells us the canoes, paddles, and life jackets are there for anyone's use.

Out on the pond, Venado tries his luck with his hand line and some cheese for bait. He sits in front of me in his dirty green polar fleece pullover that has seen the entire trail, with his new blue polar fleece hat dropping down over his eyes, as I slowly paddle around the edge of the pond.

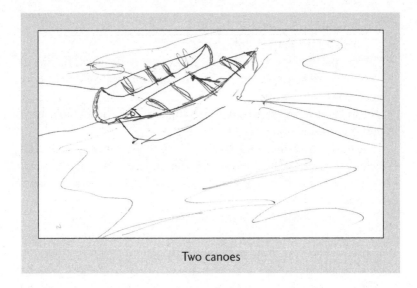

Two canoes

"Could we see a moose here?" Venado asks, pulling his hat back and looking around the quiet scene. Dark spruces and gray rocks hem the pond, here and there patches of marsh stretch into the forest.

"Maybe."

We try our luck fishing again in the morning and catch nothing but a beautiful sunrise on the water. We take it in and move on, and by mid-morning we reach the road to Rangeley. We have to go in to augment our supplies, and I explain our new plan to Venado. "We're going to buy a bunch of freeze-dried food for the 100-Mile Wilderness and mail it to ourselves in Monson, and then we'll call your mom and let her know what we need in the resupply box—no more heavy food."

As we stand by the road, hitching a ride, a car pulls over going the other way and a red-haired hiker gets out. He crosses over and stops to talk to us. When he hears that we are thru-hikers, he smiles. "Are you Venado?" he asks my son. Venado smiles, nodding. "Yeah!"

"I'm Apocalypse. I was trying to catch you down south, then I got past you."

"Oh yeah! We saw your posts in the shelter registers."

"You were with somebody else though."

"My mom. Seaweed. We heard about you, and then we missed you by one day in Harpers Ferry."

Apocalypse wants Venado's picture. He takes it with a beat-up instamatic, and I take one of him with Venado. "I'll mail you a copy when I get the film developed," Apocalypse promises. While we talk, a pickup truck pulls over. A woman at the wheel waits patiently for us to finish our goodbyes before offering us a ride into Rangeley.

Walking out of town two hours later, with bellies full of cheeseburgers and having accomplished our mission of buying and mailing several freeze-dried meals ahead to Monson, we stop at a supermarket and restock our supply of energy bars, ramen, and fuel. We buy a half dozen donuts and I bolt my three down so fast that I'm eyeing Venado's. "No way, Poppy. You ate yours." When he drops a piece of donut and sees me lunging for it, he covers it with his body, shouting, "No!" Some days I'm his father; others, I'm just another kid.

At Piazza Rock Lean-to, just north of the road, we meet up with Spoon and his gang again. Spoon's father has driven up from Cape Cod to join his son and his friends for a few days' hiking. A ridge-runner happens by, and he takes a group photo of us all. "Venado is the only one who hasn't grown a beard," someone jokes.

As is our custom, Venado and I leave the sleepy camp at dawn. Around lunchtime, we pass a hammock camper just waking up. He catches up with us later as we build thick salami sandwiches on fresh bread from town.

"Ah, what have we here?" he asks in a thick accent. He is Roni the Israeli, he tells us, "a lowly section hiker" just out taking in the easy parts. "I'm not pushing myself," he says. He calls us "ground dwellers" because we don't sleep in hammocks and he makes a comment about the high quality of our food. I offer him some, but Roni declines. "I have my own stash of goodies," he says, pulling a donut hole from a pouch hanging around his neck. "And I don't share," he says, popping the treat into his mouth.

"But we offered you a sandwich," says Venado.

"That's true," says Roni. "Okay, in that case I will share." He gives us a donut hole to split. "I also have a snack which is the best in the world."

"What?" Venado asks.

"I'm not telling. Maybe I will let you try one."

"But what is it?

"He's playing with you, Venado," I warn and head up the trail, leaving the two, who seem to be on the same food wavelength.

Venado and Roni get into a long conversation that takes up the afternoon, leaving me to walk ahead of them in silence.

"We met one guy, Jaybird," says Venado. "He hiked the trail nine times but never drank raw milk."

"Well I know people who have hiked the trail eleven times and never spoke Hebrew," says Roni. "That makes about as much sense as what you're telling me about raw milk."

I hear Venado giggling.

"Of course I am just a simple Middle Eastern-type guy," says Roni. "Maybe there is some logic to what you're saying but my brain is too small to understand it."

We're taking a rest at the ford across Orbeton Stream when Joker, Watermelon, and Zamboni catch up with us, and Joker goes on a bit of an anti-Zionist rant. Roni calls them all morons, but in such an eloquent way that they pack up and hike away in silence.

Venado sticks close to his new friend—who listens well and engages with him more than anyone else has—until Roni leaves us on the climb up Spaulding Mountain. Before he goes, he gives Venado one of his prize snacks: a mustard and onion pretzel nugget.

"Sounds disgusting," I say. "Pure chemicals."

"Poppy, it's good."

"Come on, we have a big climb and not much light left."

As darkness closes in, Spoon comes up behind us. "We gonna make it to the shelter?" I ask, looking back over my shoulder.

"Oh yeah," says Spoon and he stays right behind us, pushing us up the mountain and on to the Spaulding Mountain Lean-to in the last light of day. Joker and the rest have found space in the shelter, along with the guys with the bad dog from Vermont, and I steer Venado right past them to one of the tent sites, a bad choice. Sometime in the night I get up to pee and come back to the tent stinking of human excrement. "Oh my god, I think I stepped in somebody's shit," I realize.

"Papa!" says Venado, scolding me for cursing. I curse some more, remove my stinking boot, and toss it away from the tent. It takes me a half an hour to get it clean in the morning, but we still get away from the shelter before anyone else. Around noon, Venado and I slip off

Stepped in it

down a side trail to eat lunch at a scenic vista. We hear the crowd from Spaulding coming, and listen as they go by.

"What a relief," I say. "I was afraid they would come out here."

With only eight more miles to go, we rest a while and let the other hikers get well ahead. "I don't want any more run-ins with that dog," I tell Venado.

That night, stealth-camped by the road to Stratton, we hear something snorting out in the woods. I sit up, scrambling for a flashlight. Venado sits up next to me. "What? What?"

"I don't know." But in the instant the flashlight beam turns on, a huge bull moose with a wide rack of antlers comes blowing and charging through our camp like a freight train. I keep the beam on it.

"Holy . . . I thought it was a bear."

"Poppy, he was so close!"

"Yeah, I'm glad he didn't run over us."

When daylight comes, we christen the place Bull Moose Camp and head into Stratton, arriving just as the post office opens. With rain in the forecast, we opt for a zero and stay two nights at Susan Smith's hostel, promising to mail her copies of my books in exchange for the thirty dollars we owe her for the second night. At the store we buy a carton of MOO (Maine's Own Organic) Milk, and the carton features a photo of our dairy farmer friends from Tide Mill Farm, near home.

"Look, Poppy, it's Carly and Aaron," Venado says, turning the box for me to see the photo.

"Hey! How about that? Our pals!"

By the time we get back on the trail, Spoon and company and the bad dog boys, have surged far ahead. Venado and I, carrying only three days' food, climb toward Myron Avery Peak, devising new rhymes for our song. We camp in the cold, wet woods near four thousand feet and make a happy descent to Flagstaff Lake the next day. When we reach the lake, I suggest we hike on another three miles to the shelter, but Venado prevails upon me to camp there. A loon calls from out on the water, and under clear skies we make a big fire and kick back. "You don't seem in too big a hurry these days, Venado."

"No. I'm not attracted to the idea of going home."

"Well I am, though I get what you mean."

Venado has found a way of life that suits him fine, and he knows all the limits and restrictions that await him back in civilization.

Hiking over gentle terrain among various ponds, we arrive the next night at Pierce Pond Lean-to to find Johnny Walker there with another guy. We catch up, not having seen him since the South, and late in the evening, we hear another familiar voice.

To our mutual delight Dos XX comes around the corner and into the shelter, followed by Birch and a hiker who Venado and I have never met. "Hey! Tecolote and Venado."

"Hey Dos, Birch, and you."

"Ice." We trade shouts of joy and hugs all around. Dos XX introduces us to Ice, their new comrade, and the evening fills with an eager exchange of stories about who's been where. We jam into the crowded shelter, and Venado points to a moose-head carabiner hanging off Birch's pack. "That looks like Cowboy's," he says. "Where did you get it?"

"I found it on a tree down south," Birch tells him.

"South of Franklin?" I ask.

"Yeah."

"That's Cowboy's," says Venado. "He left it there."

"Well I'll be glad to give it back if you're still in touch with him."

"Yeah, we are."

"Amazing," I say, examining the carabiner. "I remember that."

As we hunker down for the night, Dos XX searches for a book to read. "What've we got here? *The Devil's Backbone: The Story of the Natchez Trace.*"

"Yeah, read that," I say. "My great-great-great-grandfather is buried down in Natchez. He died there of dysentery during the Civil War."

Dos XX reads us to sleep, and he and the other fast hikers linger in their bags the next morning as Venado and I make our getaway. "I'm sure they'll be passing us by lunchtime, as usual," says Venado.

"No doubt."

The lowlands have their pros and cons. Venado and I score delicious apples from a roadside tree after picking up a resupply box at Caratunk, but a few days later we hike along a swampy section of trail, walking long into dusk in search of a place to camp, and end up on a barely dry patch of leaves. A mile out of camp the next day, we come to a flooded stream and, after some minutes of exploration and consideration, accept that the only way to get across is to take off our pants and wade. It's dicey, especially for us, the shortest guys on the trail, but we make it. On the other side, Venado realizes he lost a gaiter. "It doesn't matter," he says, but I don't buy it.

"We better go back for it."

"It doesn't matter. I can get new ones," he insists.

"It does matter," I tell him. "Those gaiters cost twenty-five dollars and we're not leaving one behind. You have to go back across and get it."

Free cookies from the postmistress
at Caratunk P.O.

"Poppy, no. I don't need it."

"Yes you do, and the time you spend resisting is just going to be wasted because we're not going anywhere without that gaiter. Now come on."

Back at the stream's edge we look across and see the gaiter, hanging in a bush. Venado strips down again and wades back for it. Later we wade across a wide, shallow river and meet a man on the other side. He says he's carrying trail magic into a shelter, and he gives us sodas and candy bars that we consume on the spot. We crush the cans and put them in the side pocket of Venado's pack. Fueled by the sugar buzz, we make good time and arrive in Monson in the late afternoon.

With rain coming again, the hostels fill up quickly, but we find bunks at Shaw's, pick up our boxes of food at the post office—lightweight things like freeze-dried dinners and granola, and heavy but calorie-dense energy bars—and wander downtown for pizza. Dos XX, Birch, and Ice have landed at a combination hostel/laundromat/bar, along with Roni, who joins us for supper.

Breakfast the next morning at Shaw's proves to be one of the high points of the trail. Shaw's welcomes all comers for breakfast, no matter where they stay, and everyone, including Roni the Israeli, finds seats at the long tables before Mrs. Shaw asks, "What do you want to start?"

Everyone stares at her. "It's all you can eat," she says. "I just need to know what you want to start, two eggs, three eggs? Two sausages, three?"

"Three of everything," I say. "Eggs, bacon, and sausage," and everyone agrees.

"Okay, three of everything, for everyone. Even the little guy?"

"Yeah," says Venado, nodding emphatically.

"He's no slacker when it comes to eating," I tell her.

After we down our first plates and load up on seconds, Roni, sitting hemmed in against a wall, reaches over and takes Venado's sausages.

"Hey!" says Venado.

"Oh, didn't I tell you I steal food? Especially from children."

"That's mine!"

"And, this was your bacon," says Roni, seizing two strips off Venado's plate before the boy can stop him. "Please, go get some more. I'm hungry."

"Poppy, he took my food."

I shrug and say nothing. Venado goes for more.

Rain pours down outside, but soon after breakfast Venado and I head out into it. At the last road crossing, a sign announces that we are entering the 100-Mile Wilderness, that we should be in good condition and have at least a week's worth of food. "Well we have six days' worth," I say, and after three miles we arrive with soaked feet at Leeman Brook. Dos XX, Birch, and Ice join us soon after.

We have heard about possible flooding, and when we arrive at Little Wilson Stream the next day, we find it thundering between banks twenty-five feet apart. A narrow log spans the torrent just above some falls. Venado and I eat lunch there and consider the crossing.

High water at Little Wilson Stream

Dos XX and the others arrive and we watch them cross, straddling the log and inching along on their butts, the water roaring past beneath their feet. One of Birch's hiking poles vanishes when he accidentally throws it into the stream. Venado and I admit to each other that if he went in he would be over the falls before anyone could get to him. We've come so far and taken so many chances already, but this one looks like more than we can handle, worn out as we are.

"It's too much risk," I say. We wave goodbye to our old friends, hike two miles back, and take a detour along the road. In transit, we stop two men in a truck and ask directions. The men have a detailed map of the area and offer us a look at it. I find a line marking a trail that will get us back to the AT and take a picture of it with my iPhone.

"Your name's Garrett, isn't it? Garrett Conover?" I ask, looking at one of the men. "You run trips up to Labrador." The man says yes, that's who he is. "You know, I have a picture of your wife, Alexandra, paddling a birch-bark canoe hanging in my cabin. You know that picture, Venado? That's this guy's wife."

Walking along a quiet road, I'm telling Venado about the sort of trips Garrett and his wife run up in Labrador—skiing and pulling toboggans across the tundra. Distracted, Venado asks if he is still going to be a thru-hiker after taking this detour.

"Of course," I tell him. "Road walks are permitted when the trail in impassable." I'm writing to Laurie Potteiger at the Appalachian Trail Conservancy to confirm this, when we come upon a man in a little truck pulled off to the side of the road. We wave and he asks where we're going. We tell him and he gives us directions to a shelter along the way. "It's just out there in the woods. I don't think the owners'll mind if you use it." I repeat the directions carefully. "That's right. I'd offer you a ride," he says, "but if you're hiking the trail you probably wouldn't want it."

"Right," says Venado, smiling.

I ask his name. "Dentremont," the man says.

"Do your people come from Pubnico?" I ask.

"Yes, they're all from over there in Nova Scotia."

"Hah, Acadian. Our ancestor Charles de la Tour was governor of Acadia in the sixteen-thirties. We're probably distantly related then."

"How about that?" the man laughs. "Well good luck."

Walking along I mention to Venado how much it feels like we're home—and how short the days are getting. "I don't think we're going to make it to the trail," I venture. "We better find that shelter." And we do.

Following the map photo on my iPhone, we strike the trail north of Little and Big Wilson Streams the next morning and head up a steep climb. "Oh man, I thought we were all done with these Myron Avery rock scrambles," I complain.

"You call them 'Myron Avery Specials,'" Venado reminds me.

The night promises clear skies and plummeting temperatures, so we pass up the shelter at Chairback Gap and descend to the West Branch of the Pleasant River, planning to cross in the morning.

At dawn on October 3, we slip on our camp shoes—me in my crocs, and Venado in his moccasins—and roll up our pants; we've each

Road walk

found a sturdy stick for balance, and, holding hands, we step into the wide shallow river.

"Oh my god, that's cold."

"Poppy, this is freezing!"

We move carefully, slowly, through the icy water, and arrive on the other side almost in shock. Venado stumbles up to a log and sits down. "Poppy, my feet are so cold."

"Oh my god yeah, oh that is soooo cold," I say, sitting down next to him. He's crying.

"I'm crying too, honey." I turn and straddle the log. "Come here," I say. "Tuck your feet up under my shirt." When those feet hit my belly

I jump. "Wow, cold. Let's get our boots on and walk. That'll warm us up." It takes half a mile before we stop talking about our feet.

We find moose sign, tracks, and scat on the trail all up through Gulf Hagas and discover switchbacks as we ascend White Cap Mountain. "What happened here?" I ask. "Somebody did away with a Myron Avery Special."

"Yeah, you can see the old trail," says Venado, and sure enough it leads straight up the mountain. We take the welcome switchbacks to the top of White Cap, the last big mountain before Katahdin, which we see seventy-three miles away. I take a picture of Venado with our goal in the background. "Now let me take yours," he says, and he snaps a picture of me in the late afternoon sun.

We stealth-camp near a stream on the way down the mountain and hike into East Branch Lean-to for breakfast. We manage to ford the East Branch of the Pleasant River dry-footed and make incredible time over to Potaywadjo Stream—a twenty-three-mile day. The only other person we meet at the shelter is Boston Bones. He's an epileptic, and a survivor of a bad motorcycle accident and a near-fatal car accident. He explains where all the steel rods and plates are in his body, and how he got his trail name. We tell him he's the most amazing hiker we've met. "You're more of a miracle than us," I say.

As the sun sets, we settle into our bags, just the three of us in the quiet spacious shelter.

"They say they close the mountain on October fifteenth," Bones tells us. "You think we're gonna make it?"

"Sure," says Venado.

I shrug. "We'll see. But that's not the main thing right now. The question is whether to go to White House Landing for a one-pound burger, or hike another twenty miles tomorrow."

"I know what I'm doing," says Bones. "I'm having a burger."

Venado agrees, but I make no commitment.

When we get to the fork in the trail the next morning, Venado wants to go for the burger. "Poppy, can we please?" I prevail upon him to hike on. We have heard stories about the White House owner scolding people for infractions of all sorts of arbitrary rules. "It's too early, Venado. We'll be waiting all day for a burger, and I don't want anybody yelling at me."

We continue another half mile. "Poppy, are you sure you want to go on?"

"No, I'm not," I admit. "The thought of that burger is burning in my mind." I sit down and pull out our guidebook. "Let's think about this." I thumb through the worn and dirt-smudged pages that cover the trail we are on, mumbling calculations. "If we go for burgers, we can make it to Wadleigh Stream tonight, but then we'd have a twenty-mile day to Hurd Brook. You up for that?"

"Sure."

So we double back to the White House, following Bones's footprints from the fork in the trail to a dock on the shore of Pemadumcook Lake. Across the lake we can see a lodge, and a little speedboat at another dock.

"Poppy, here's the horn. Can I blow it?"

"Sure."

Venado makes a short blast and we look across the lake. A sign by the horn tells us we only need to blow it once—other hikers have also warned us not to blow it twice—and that it may take some time before someone comes over with the boat. I make tea for myself and hot chocolate for Venado, while he builds a little fort out of sticks, turning a moose hoofprint into a shelter for elves. After an hour, a man comes across for us. "Why didn't you blow the horn?" he asks.

"We did."

"We never heard it. We saw you over here and you stayed so long we figured you must want to come over."

On the way back to the lodge, he introduces himself to us: He is Bill Ware, owner of White House Landing, and he never scolds us at all.

Bones, Venado, and I wait with anticipation at a table in the lodge, smelling our burgers cook. The famous one-pound burgers don't stand a chance against us—as soon as they hit the table we tear through them. With the first course finished, the taste of sweet fat still lingering under my tongue, I look at Venado. "I could almost eat another."

"Me too."

"Let's have dessert instead, some of that pumpkin pie."

We top off our supplies with a couple of ramen noodle packets from the hiker box and head for Wadleigh Stream. It starts to rain and we reach the shelter just in time to get the last two spots on the sleeping platform. People keep rolling in, though, until every available space under cover has a prostrate hiker on it. When Venado and I leave at dawn, we shake awake two guys lying in the dirt in front of the platform.

"Hey, you guys want to get up here? There's room."

"Oh, thanks, man," one of them says, and drags his bag up onto the platform.

Venado and I walk along a carpet of brightly colored fallen leaves, past cliffs shrouded in mist.

"Isn't this cool, Venado?"

"Yeah."

"I would take a picture, but I don't think it'll come out."

We hike without stopping. The rain patters on the fallen leaves, turning them all shiny red and yellow, and though the trail presents no mountains for us to climb, the wet and muddy ground makes for hard going. We arrive within sight of Hurd Brook at the end of the day and spot Blue-ish and Seaweed standing on the north bank waving and calling to us. Venado leaps from boulder to boulder across the brook and into his mother's arms. She takes his pack and we walk up the hill to the shelter.

I spot Roni sitting on a log. "Oh Roni, we are going to kill you in the food wars, man. We have got the goods. You are going to be so envious." Laughing, I turn to Seaweed. "Speaking of which, where are the goodies?"

"Back in the car," she says. Three and a half miles away.

"The car?"

"You can go get them if you want."

I stand there staring at her.

"I brought you some veggie wraps," she says.

"You left them in the car?"

"Daddy, calm down," says Blue-ish, stepping between Seaweed and me.

"Veggie wraps are good," says Venado.

"I would trade peanut butter for some veggie wrap," says Roni.

"That's not what I had in mind," I say to Roni as Seaweed hands me a veggie wrap.

I would trade for veggie wraps!

I accept it and eat it quietly. My wife scratches my head. "It'll be okay," she tells me. I start to respond, but she gives me a look that suggests I oughtn't.

"Calories," I mumble.

"Drop it."

We move on to other topics, plans for the following days: the hike to the Birches tomorrow and the climb the following day.

"How's the weather looking?" I ask.

"Iffy."

15

KATAHDIN

After breakfast on October 8, Venado and his sister romp through the woods the three and a half miles out to the car. Seaweed and I follow, talking easily; I never mention the goodies. When we get to our car, Venado and I shed our packs for the last time.

Therese Lussier and her husband, Dave, new friends from our Barbarian Utopia page, have come down from Houlton to meet us, and they greet us with a gift: a heavy loaf of pumpkin bread. Standing by the road, talking, Venado and I demolish most of it. We take pictures and Therese buys the kids candy bars at the Abol Bridge store. Seaweed loads us up with more high-calorie goods and Venado and I take off, slack-packing the last ten miles to the Birches, the campsite at the foot of Katahdin. We take our time. Venado makes up a song, borrowing the tune and some of the words from a sea chanty we heard in the movie *Master and Commander.*

"We entered into Maryland, not sure if we would ma-ake it, with no bears or rattlesnakes, only the wind and the rai-ai-n. Long we've hiked in the snow and the rain, now we're heading home again."

"Don't forget your old trail mates, Falalalala la la," I sing, finishing the line.

Seaweed has a campsite reserved, and after an easy hike along the West Branch of the Penobscot River, we arrive and help her and Blue-ish set up the tents. We wander over to the park headquarters to sign in. The ranger fills out Venado's thru-hiker paperwork, to be mailed to Laurie Potteiger at the Appalachian Trail Conservancy. On the porch of the park office sits a scale model of Mount Katahdin, and the kids pore over it. They find the Hunt Trail, and follow it up to the top of the mountain. "How far is it?"

"Five miles."

"Can we go on the Knife Edge?"

"Not likely. It's supposed to be quite windy. Imagine getting blown off there," I say, pointing to the sharp-edged ridge that rises up to the summit.

"Ahhhhh," says Venado imitating a long fall.

"Besides," I remind him, "it's not the Appalachian Trail."

Coming out of the office, we hear the nearby parking lot buzzing with energy and walk over to find it full of people we know. Dos XX, Birch, Ice, Giant, DB, and a half dozen others have just come off the mountain. Standing around in hats and jackets, surrounded by the gold and red leaves of the autumnal forest, bright in the late afternoon sun, they all offer Venado enthusiastic congratulations. Birch gives him his hiking pole. "Here, Venado, you want this?"

"Yeah!" says Venado, taking the well-worn pole whose mate disappeared back in Little Wilson Stream.

"How was it?" I ask Dos XX after introducing everyone to Blue-ish and Seaweed.

"Oh man, you couldn't see shit; it was a total whiteout up there. If it's like this tomorrow, don't go, wait a day."

"We have to go tomorrow," I tell him. "We have a wedding on Sunday that can't be missed." But others echo Dos XX's description of the mountain, giving us some concern. Huff-N-Puff, who we met at points along the trail, takes me aside. "Listen," he says, "it's the worst at the rebar; once you get past that it gets easier."

The weather report posted at the ranger station calls for a Class III day on October 9, with some trails closed. It does not look good, but

At the foot of Katahdin

along with the others planning to summit the following day, we hang on to hope.

A heavily bearded hiker approaches Venado and asks, with a Spanish accent, "Did I hear this right, did you hike the trail?"

"Yep," says Venado.

The man introduces himself as Red Stick; he asks Venado's name. Venado tells him.

"Venado? Like deer?"

"Yeah," says Venado, nodding.

"And where do you live, Venado?"

"Maine."

"Maine?"

"Uh huh," says Venado. "Born and raised in Maine."

Red Stick turns on his video camera. "I want to interview you—is that okay?" he asks, looking at Venado and me. We both nod okay.

"So Venado, tell me about your Appalachian Trail thru-hike."

"Um, what do you want me to tell you about it?"

"Oh whatever you want to tell me, your experience: How have you been? When do you start? All that."

"Well, we started in Georgia . . . well, we did it all different, but all in one year. We did Harpers Ferry, West Virginia, to Vermont, and then Georgia to Harpers Ferry, and then, now we're doing Vermont to Maine, and now we're at Katahdin."

"So how was it? How was the trail in general for you?"

"What does that mean?"

"I mean, was it difficult? Was it easy?"

"Well it's the easiest trail in the country, so for starters, it's a good one." Venado pauses searching for words. "Well it's not really *difficult.*"

"It's not?"

"Yeah," Venado shrugs assent. "Well, there's Myron Avery Specials—they take you straight up the rocks. My father calls 'em that because Myron Avery is the guy who made the trail."

"Right."

"Benton MacKaye envisioned it, and Myron Avery built it."

"So tell me about sleeping in the woods," Red Stick asks. "Do you like it? Do you get scared?"

"I like it."

"Of course you like it; you love it, right?"

"Yeah. I wouldn't be out here anymore if I didn't like it."

"How old are you?"

"Eight."

"Okay so tell me, what do you miss when you're on the trail."

"Nothing," says Venado, staring into the camera, awaiting the next question.

"So being one day from the summit, how do you feel?"

"Umm . . . well, not great. I don't really want to get off the trail."

"Well, you have to go home and go to school."

"I'm homeschooled."

"Cool, I like that. Well, there's other trails. Do you plan to hike other trails?"

Venado explains our plans to build a birch-bark canoe, and possibly hike, bike, and canoe the Lewis and Clark Trail.

"And what's your father's name?"

"Tecolote."

"Can you call him over here?"

"Papa!"

I walk over and Red Stick records my quick synopsis of the experience.

"I'm so amazed," says Red Stick.

"Yeah, he's actually the only one of us who's hiked the whole thing."

"You should be so proud of him."

"Well, I'm also relieved, because let me tell ya, shepherding an eight-year-old across twenty-two thousand miles of, you know, sometimes risky terrain has been a lot to think about, man. But yeah, I'm proud of him."

Red Stick overlooks my overstatement of the mileage and wraps up the interview. "Remember Venado," he says, "when you reach the top of the mountain, then you begin to climb!"

"Huh?"

"Khalil Gibran."

For the last time on the trail, we recite the litany of shelters and campsites for all our friends: two hundred names—Ed Garvey to Kid Gore, Springer to David Lesser, and Stratton Pond to the Birches. It takes a while, and when we finish, we part company and Red Stick promises to meet us on the summit the next day.

I share a tent with Blue-ish. Venado shares the other with his mother, and we wake up early on the seven-month anniversary of beginning our hike, wondering if we can reach the summit. Frost covers the windows of our car, and we all shiver.

"Yah, yah, yah, let's go go go," I holler, dancing in the chill air as I heat milk for our granola and water for coffee and cocoa. By seven-thirty we are ready to go, and we begin the march. As we're crossing the parking lot, two guys come up beside me, one of them smiling. It takes a moment.

"KlifyBoy! What the hell?"

"We figured we'd come summit with you. This is my friend Bob." We stop and make introductions all around.

"Honey, do you remember KlifyBoy? He was with me the first time you and I met, back in nineteen-ninety."

"No."

"Well he doesn't remember you either, but you were both there, I promise."

Our group of six begins the trek up the mountain, groping across ice-glazed rocks, wondering all the time how bad it will get. After the first mile, we begin to meet people who have turned back, Johnny Walker and his friend among them.

"We stealth-camped in the park," he tells us. "And then we headed up at about three o'clock this morning. We've been up all night, but we couldn't do it. It's crazy up there; the wind is roaring!"

As we near the upper limit of the trees, we feel the wind, gusting to forty-five miles per hour, according to the weather report, but it feels like more. When we reach the rebar, the most difficult section of the climb, where hikers have to rely on iron bars set into the rock for footholds and handholds, the wind screams like nothing we've ever experienced.

Before beginning the technical climb, we stop and prepare, adding layers and tightening parkas and wind pants. As soon as we start climbing over the exposed boulders the full force of the wind hits us. In the lead, I can feel it tearing me off the rock. I have to hang on tight, and I wonder how the kids will handle it. Blue-ish, just behind me, throws in the towel when the first big blast hits her. "No, no," she hollers and begins climbing back down. She finds shelter below and lets the others go up. KlifyBoy, Bob, Seaweed, and Venado make it past the first difficult spot and we hold a conference in the lee of another boulder, shouting above the wind.

"We can give Blue-ish's wind pants to Venado, and you and her can go back," I say to Seaweed.

"No, Papa. We can't do it," says Venado.

I look at him. "Are you sure? Huff-n-Puff says it gets easier past the rebar. Do you wanna try?"

"No, Papa. It's too windy."

"I don't need to go," says Bob.

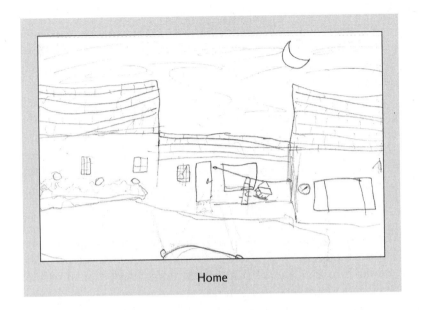

Home

Only KlifyBoy and I have yet to concede the effort. We look at each other.

"You want to try?" I ask.

"Sure."

"Okay, Seaweed, are you okay with KlifyBoy and me heading for the summit? I think we can do it."

"Sure."

So we all retreat to the tree line. I take a token from everyone and then look at Venado. "Venado, you have done everything you can, within the margins of safety and sometimes beyond, to pass every white blaze between Georgia and Katahdin. I'm calling this a thru-hike. The sign up there is just the cherry on top, and we'll come collect it another day." We all hug, and KliffyBoy and I head for the summit.

We return late in the afternoon, looking played out.

"How was it?" a woman in the campground asks.

I take out my water bottle, half filled with ice.

"Cold," says the woman.

"I don't think it would have worked for you, Venado." I tell my son. "The wind up there just sucks the life outta ya, and the return would have been dicey."

We linger long together at the foot of the mountain, its peak obscured by clouds. "I'd like to see Red Stick," I say. "He was up there; we saw him headed for the summit." But we have to leave before our new friend returns.

At the Katahdin Diner in Millinocket, they have a tradition of each year's class of thru-hikers signing tiles that then replace blanks on the diner's ceiling. Venado signs a ceiling tile bearing the names of many others he has shared the trail with over the last seven months, and after a hearty meal, we drive home in darkness. We arrive with packs still full of trail food and water drawn from springs on the way up Katahdin, but the trail is done. We did it.

The following summer, the whole family and a friend accompany Venado to the summit of Katahdin on a clear and windless day. Probing for some sense of completion, I ask Venado how it feels to finally touch the sign, but he shrugs.

"I don't get it," he says. "I already did the trail."

Acknowledgements

Hundreds of people helped make Venado's walk and this book possible, but foremost among them is Regina Grabrovac (Seaweed), without whom we would have been lost. And thanks to all our collective family members for supporting us one way or another, particularly Pidge Molyneaux, who bought a lot of gear for her grandchildren, Oona Molyneaux for running our resupply when we really needed it, and Paulette Grab for being generally great.

Among the more than 500 fans who lifted our spirits via our "Barbarian Utopia" Facebook page, Chris Scanlan, Therese Lussier, and Tammy Lee deserve mention for their great participation, as does Laurie Potteiger of the Appalachian Trail Conservancy.

A list of folks who helped us along the way could really snowball, but I would like to extent a particular thanks to our couchsurfer.org hosts Kimbi and Karl Hagen in Atlanta, and Adam Weber in Pennsylvania, as well as Sonia Lipson in Boston, whose couch we have surfed a long way. Thanks to Marie Celeste Parham, Rachel Bereson Lachow, Breeze, Robin Rieske, Jeff Butt, and Cliff Hall for your contributions to the cause. A shoutout, too, to the Piedmont Appalachian Trail Hikers, and the Appalachian Mountain Club.

Ben Pasamanick and Tony Williams both offered valuable feedback on the manuscript, and Larry Anderson provided me with a copy of his thorough biography of Benton MacKaye. Thanks to you all, and to the many, many who helped us and cheered us on.